THE BOOK OF MAGICAL HERBS

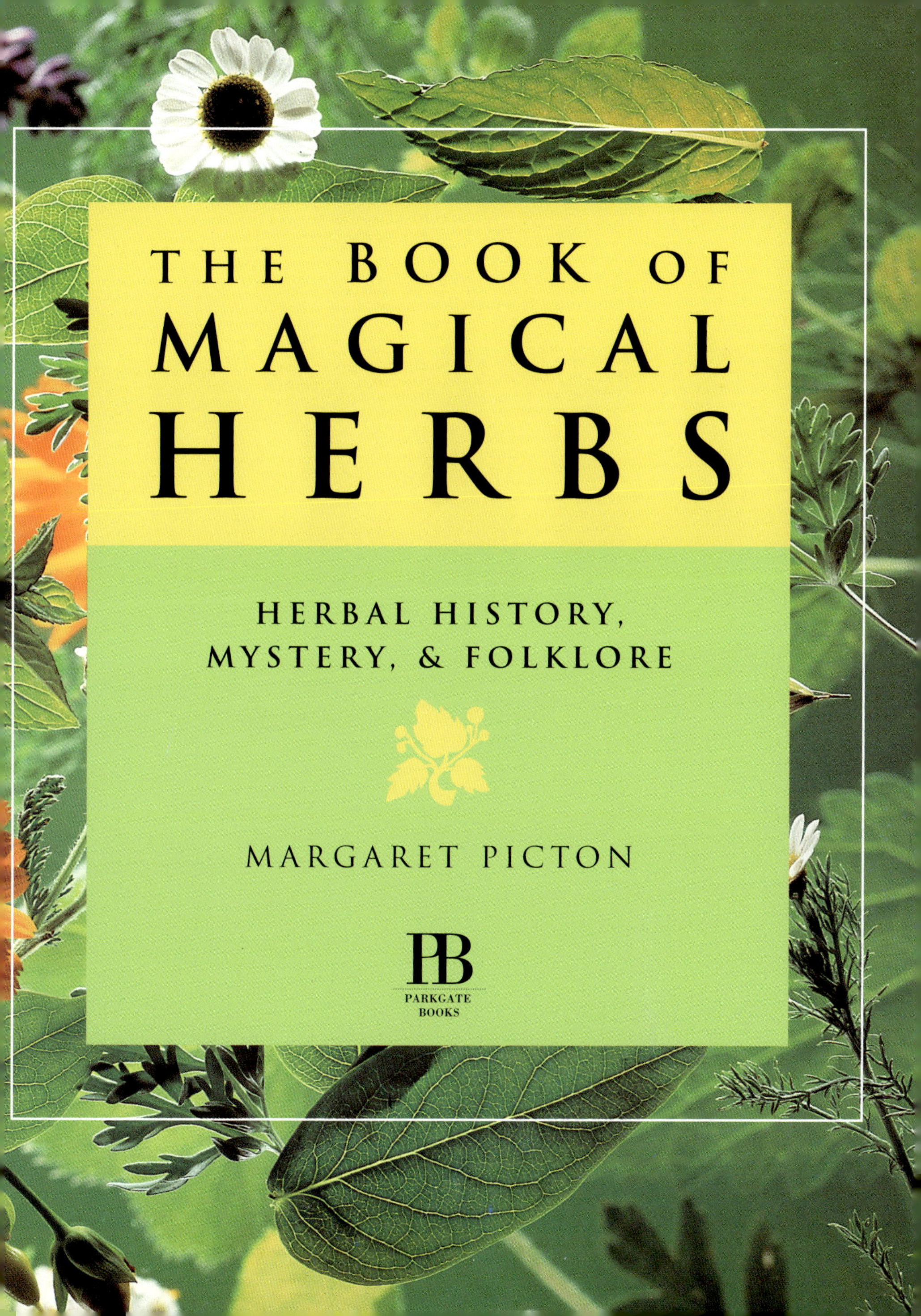

THE BOOK OF MAGICAL HERBS

HERBAL HISTORY, MYSTERY, & FOLKLORE

MARGARET PICTON

PB
PARKGATE BOOKS

A QUARTO BOOK

First published in 2000 by
Parkgate Books
London House, Great Eastern Wharf, Parkgate Road,
London SW11 4NQ

ISBN 1-902616-20-0

Conceived, designed, and produced by
Quarto Publishing plc
The Old Brewery
6 Blundell Street
London N7 9BH

QUAR.HHMF

Editor: *Michelle Pickering*
Art editor & designer: *Rebecca Adams*
Assistant art director: *Penny Cobb*
Illustrator: *John Woodcock*
Picture researcher: *Laurent Boubounelle*
Indexer: *Dorothy Frame*

Art director: *Moira Clinch*
Publisher: *Piers Spence*

Manufactured by *Regent Publishing Services Ltd, Hong Kong*
Printed by *Leefung-Asco Printers Ltd, China*

NOTE

The author, publisher, and copyright holder have made every reasonable effort to ensure that the recipes and formulas in this book are safe when used as instructed, but assume no responsibility for any injury or damage caused or sustained while using them. This book is not intended as a substitute for the advice of a health care professional.

CONTENTS

INTRODUCTION 6

SACRED & PROTECTIVE

BAY 14
YARROW 20
ANGELICA 24
GARLIC 28
TARRAGON 34
CHIVES 36
MINT 40
CHERVIL 44
CHAMOMILE 46
FENNEL 52
WORMWOOD 56
RUE 58
BORAGE 62
DILL 66

LOVE & DEATH

ROSEMARY 72
MARJORAM 78
PARSLEY 82
CORIANDER 88
LAVENDER 90
SWEET BASIL 96
THYME 102
BERGAMOT 108
SAGE 112
TANSY 118
MARIGOLD 120

INDEX 126
CREDITS 128

INTRODUCTION

Can all your tap'stries, or your pictures, show
More beauties, than in herbs and flowers do grow?

Abraham Cowley, 17th-century poet

THIS BOOK RECORDS OUR FASCINATION WITH THE HERBAL MAGIC, mysteries, and customs that have enriched the annals of folk legend throughout the ages. It recounts sacred myths, secular fables, magical rites, and time-honored superstitious beliefs and customs, all of which helped early man and woman to understand the world in which they lived as they sought to control their destiny and well-being by physiocratic means.

Ancient legacy

The almost mysterious healing power of herbs and their ability to ease pain can be traced back to the very beginning of history, when early cradles of civilization instinctively experimented with plants. They discovered, by trial and error, locally grown herbs that were effective in treating their ailments, and this knowledge was passed from one generation to another by word of mouth and practical teaching. Artifacts from many cultures, such as tomb paintings, frescoes, bas-reliefs, bronzes, and cuneiform tablets, recorded the importance of herbs to these early peoples.

Herbal healing

Ancient herbals and medical treatises described plants and their healing properties, and herbal lore and culture evolved with usage. Medieval monasteries became centers of herbal healing. They founded hospitals and had separate physic gardens where the monks grew a wide variety of plants to make the potions, oils, and ointments they needed to treat the sick. The hedgerows and woodlands provided the plants needed by the country housewife for her herbal healing. During the 16th and 17th centuries, many

A modern herb garden based on a traditional geometric design.

famous herbals were published to help housewives in the correct identification and use of herbs. William Turner, a doctor and priest who became known as the father of English botany, wrote *A New Herball* c. 1551, and John Gerard's work *The Herball* was published in 1597. John Parkinson, who was apothecary to King James I, wrote *Paradisus* in 1629, and this prolific period ended with Nicholas Culpeper's best-selling and influential *The English Physician*, c. 1653. Culpeper devoted much of his time to the study of astrology and medicine. He worked as an apothecary in London, and gave free treatment to the many poor people who came to him for advice. His legacy to future generations consisted of a huge collection of herbal remedies, some of which are as useful today as they were over 300 years ago.

Nicholas Culpeper (1616–1654) linked herbs to astrological signs.

Magical herbs

Many herbs were endowed with magical properties. The Anglo-Saxons had nine sacred herbs, which they used to keep themselves safe from all kinds of evil influences, and with which they made a cure-all magic salve. Herbs were carried in the hand, worn as amulets, or hung over doorways, windows, and beds as charms against witchcraft, demons, nightmares, and disease. Others were boiled together to make protective potions and drunk. Fennel had a benign anti-witch reputation. The herb was suspended from rafters on Midsummer Eve (June 23rd) as a

Fennel

Thyme

good luck talisman, and its seeds were pushed into the keyholes of haunted houses to keep malignant forces away. Thyme was strongly associated with magic, witchcraft, and violent death. It was a constituent of a magical ointment that purported to allow people to see fairies. Some herbs had hallucinogenic properties, and witches added them to their magic brews to encourage an increased state of susceptibility in their clients. Wormwood was one herb beloved of witches, because it made people have double vision.

Witches were thought to use bay to make their flying broomsticks.

Harvesting herbs

According to ancient lore, herbs were most effective if sown or planted during the first or second quarter of the moon. There was a strong belief that the properties of plants were more potent when they were gathered at night, and Saxon people were advised to harvest herbs at dusk, "when day and night divide."

Many curious customs surrounded the picking of herbs. The Druids dressed in white linen robes for the task and went barefooted as they cut their precious plants with a gold blade. It was thought to be particularly effective to harvest herbs during, or just after, a full moon. Country folk gathered herbs in the left hand and never faced into the wind or looked backward during the task. They talked to the plants as they cut, and left any herbs that were dropped on the ground because it was thought that their goodness had seeped back into the earth. Some herbs could only be cut with certain implements. It was not thought right, for example, to cut herbs with tools made from iron.

A fragrant feast

The harvest was dried for winter use and for making potpourris and perfumed bags to keep the house smelling fresh and fragrant. In Tudor times, large houses had elaborate herb gardens, usually contained within clipped yew hedges or surrounded by low borders of contrasting herbs pruned to give a "knotted" effect. Each manor house had a still room where herbs were dried, pounded, and distilled to make a range of aromatic products, including sweet-scented waters, flower syrups, and perfumed candles.

The floors of houses and churches were covered with sweet-smelling herbs and rushes. These fragrant carpets gave off a delightful perfume that helped to mask unpleasant odors. Some herbs also served as efficient insect repellents and others helped to combat disease. Strewing floors with herbs was thought to be particularly important in times of plague, and from the 17th century onward, law courts were similarly treated to protect the judiciary from contagious diseases.

Bay and citrus Christmas wreath

Herbs today

Today, herbs still retain some of their ancient significance. Bay is one of the evergreens traditionally associated with Christmas and is often a component of seasonal wreaths, and rosemary is linked with remembrance. Children, often unwittingly, keep alive herbal lore in the games they play, such as "Ring Around the Rosey," which re-enacts the symptoms of the plague. Fragrant herbs are capable of provoking strong feelings, reminding us of childhood memories and special vacations by the sea or in the country, and this passion has been expressed in verse and prose throughout the ages. This book will show you how life can be enhanced by rediscovering the mystical, legendary powers of herbs for yourself.

Rosemary

HERBAL RECIPES

This book contains many herbal recipes to charm, soothe, heal, and protect, and the treatment methods used include:

Marjoram

Infusions

These are made by pouring boiling water over fresh or dried herbs. Let the herbs steep in the water for about 10 minutes, stirring occasionally, then strain off the liquid. Infusions are most suitable for leaves and flowers. They can be used hot or cold, but should always be freshly made.

Decoctions

A decoction is generally used for the hard parts of plants, such as roots and seeds, which must be boiled or simmered to extract their healing properties. Place the herb and some water in a saucepan and bring to a boil. Simmer for at least 10 minutes. Cool, then strain the liquid, squeezing the herbs in order to extract all the juices.

Compresses

These are made by soaking a cloth in an herbal infusion and applying it directly to an affected area. Both hot and cold compresses can be used, depending on the complaint being treated.

Poultices

These are made by enclosing fresh herbs in a cloth, immersing the pad briefly in boiling water, and applying the squeezed hot poultice externally. Keep the poultice moist by dipping it briefly into the hot water periodically.

CAUTION

It should be remembered that self-treatment with herbal remedies should only be attempted for very minor ailments. If you have previously experienced any kind of allergic reaction to medicines and skin products, always seek advice before experimenting with the recipes in this book, and stop treatment immediately if you feel worse.

reviving

hallowed

refreshing

SACRED &

invigorating

healing

medicinal

inspirational

holy

flavorsome

PROTECTIVE

mystical

Wild and cultivated **herbs** are the oldest method of alleviating pain, treating symptoms, and curing disease, and early civilizations revered **herbs** for their mystical healing properties. **Herbs** were thought to be important ingredients of witches' spells and potions, and the hallucinogenic effect of some **herbs** deepened people's belief in their magical powers. **Herbs** were featured in religious festivals and were often dedicated to or named in honor of ancient gods and Christian saints. Particular plants were even thought to offer sacred protection from plague, lightning, and evil forces.

BAY

Laurus nobilis

What is there in the universal Earth
More lovely than a wreath from the bay tree?

John Keats, *To the Ladies who Saw Me Crowned*, 1817

inspirational

holy

flavorsome

PROTECTIVE

mystical

Wild and cultivated **herbs** are the oldest method of alleviating pain, treating symptoms, and curing disease, and early civilizations revered **herbs** for their mystical healing properties. **Herbs** were thought to be important ingredients of witches' spells and potions, and the hallucinogenic effect of some **herbs** deepened people's belief in their magical powers. **Herbs** were featured in religious festivals and were often dedicated to or named in honor of ancient gods and Christian saints. Particular plants were even thought to offer sacred protection from plague, lightning, and evil forces.

BAY

Laurus nobilis

What is there in the universal Earth
More lovely than a wreath from the bay tree?

John Keats, *To the Ladies who Saw Me Crowned*, 1817

THE ANCIENTS VENERATED THIS SACRED HERB, WHICH WAS USED IN MANY PAGAN RITES AND CEREMONIES. It was dedicated to Apollo, whom legend tells us fell in love with the nymph Daphne. As she fled from his embraces, she was transformed into a bay tree. Thereafter, Apollo wore a wreath of bay leaves on his head and exhorted his followers to do likewise, as a symbol of his protection against the powers of evil. Apollo also built a temple of bay branches at Delphi in Greece. Later, a more permanent temple of stone was constructed there, but bay was still used to cover the inner sanctum, and every ninth year it was the custom to erect a bower of bay branches in the forecourt.

The ancient Greeks held a festival to celebrate peace and victory, called the Feast of the Laurel-bearing. During the procession, Theban maidens crowned with bay sang hymns of praise to Apollo. People believed that this magical herb allowed prophets to foretell coming events. The oracles at Delphi, who consulted the gods, chewed bay leaves and shook a nearby bay tree before going into a trance and being inspired with the gift of prophecy.

Bay in modern times is a symbol of excellence in literature and the arts. The phrase "to look to one's laurels" means that success in any field has to be maintained, and "to rest on one's laurels" implies satisfaction with what has already been achieved. Bay is the birthday flower for July 14th. In flower symbolism, the tree represents glory and the leaf stands for unchanging affection. According to the 17th-century herbalist Nicholas Culpeper, the bay is a tree of the sun and under the influence of Leo.

SACRED PROTECTION

I have seen the wicked in great power
And spreading himself like a green bay tree.

The Bible, Psalms 37:35

People believed that bay offered protection because of its connection with Apollo. Always associated with witchcraft and good luck charms, bay was believed to banish all evil spirits. Branches of bay were hung in churches in medieval times to welcome good fairies and elves. Country folk believed that bay was a favorite wood for witches' broomsticks, the wooden steeds that carried them through the air on their midnight journeys.

It was thought that the aromatic odor of bay helped to drive away infections, and superstitious folk would keep a bay leaf in their mouths whenever there was a plague. During one such pestilence, the Roman Emperor Claudius was advised to transfer his court to Laurentum, a city celebrated for the large number of bay trees growing there.

Throughout history, there has been a belief that bay offers protection against thunder and lightning. The Emperor Tiberius was reported to be so afraid of lightning that he crept under his bed and covered his head with bay whenever there was a thunderstorm.

If a bay tree died, it was thought to presage a death in the family or a national disaster. According to contemporary records, all the bay trees in Rome withered before the death of Nero. If bay wood burned on the hearth with a loud crack, it was considered a sign of good luck. However, if the bay only smoldered on the fire, the signs were less favorable.

✤ Plant a bay tree close to your house for protection from thunder and lightning. ✤

✤ Put a bay leaf under your pillow for inspiration and to dream of the future. ✤

✤ Wear a baby's tooth or a cherry stone (traditionally a wolf's tooth) wrapped in a bay leaf that has been picked during August to hear kind words spoken about you. ✤

✤ Take a bay tree with you when moving to a new house, so that good luck is not left behind. ✤

CELEBRATION

Oh, beautiful Bay, I worship thee—
I homage thy wreath, I cherish thy tree,
And of all the chaplets Fame may deal
'Tis only to this one I would kneel.

Eliza Cook, 19th-century poet

IN ANCIENT GREECE AND ROME, wreaths of bay were used to crown distinguished scholars, poets, winning athletes, and triumphant generals. This herb was associated with success and honor, so letters telling the news of victorious battles were wrapped in bay leaves, and their bearers carried a branch of bay. Bay was used to decorate the mail coaches carrying the news of the British triumph over the French at the Battle of Waterloo. Throughout history, this herb has been depicted on busts, coins, and works of art. It decorated the palace gates of the Caesars and those of the high pontiffs of Rome, and Julius Caesar is said to have valued greatly the honor accorded by the Senate that allowed him to wear a crown of bay. This helped to hide his baldness, a feature the Romans considered a deformity.

During the festival of Saturnalia, a pagan forerunner of Christmas, the Romans decorated their homes with bay. Gradually, over the years, bay became one of the evergreens associated with the Christmas season. Bay was traditionally exchanged between friends at the New Year to symbolize the hope that the coming year would be as full of good fortune as the bay tree. In Greece, during the festival of Holy Saturday (celebrated on the day before Easter Sunday), bay leaves were spread on the floor of churches.

✤ Wrap dried figs in bay leaves to give to friends at New Year's. ✤

✤ Decorate doorways in your home with bay leaves for good luck when a wedding is being celebrated. ✤

✤ Break a bay twig in two and give one half to your lover to ensure faithfulness. ✤

COMFORT

In Roman times, bay leaves were used in hot baths to ease aching limbs. In folk medicine, the juice of bay berries was used to treat snake bites, bee and wasp stings, and infectious diseases. It was believed that if seven bay berries were given to a woman in labor, they would ensure a quick delivery. Bay berries were sometimes eaten to try to end an unwanted pregnancy. Bay leaves broken upward from a branch were used to induce vomiting; leaves broken downward were thought to have a purging effect.

Bay was one of the herbs burned as a household antiseptic and insecticide. It was a popular strewing plant for covering floors, particularly in Roman times, and was put into flour and packed around licorice and dried figs to discourage the weevil beetle. Roman cooks pounded black bay berries with other seeds and herbs to make a pungent sauce to accompany meat.

The oil takes away the marks of the skin and flesh caused by bruises, falls, etc.

Nicholas Culpeper, *The English Physician*, c. 1653

✤ Drop a few bay leaves into the cooking liquid when boiling cauliflower and cabbage to reduce the pungent smell. ✤

✤ Soak in a hot bath with a bag of bay leaves to relieve rheumatic pain. ✤

✤ Relax with a facial steam bath using bay leaves, chamomile flowers, rose petals, and rosemary steeped in boiling water. ✤

✤ Make a fragrant sleep pillow using dried bay, bergamot, and chamomile. ✤

HONEY mead

"Take a quart [2 pints/1 liter] of honey and 7 quarts [14 pints/7 liters] of water; of bay, rosemary, and hyssope of each a sprigg. Mix them together and boyle them halfe an houre, and then let it stand till it be clear. Then put it up in a pot with a tap, and set new yeast on it, and let it worke untill it be clear, then bottle it up and let it be two months ould before you drink it. It may be drunk before, but ye keeping it soe long makes it brisker."

Martha Washington's *Booke of Cookery*, 16th century

YARROW

Achillea millefolium

Thou pretty herb of the Venus tree
Thy true name it is yarrow.
Who is my true bosom friend to be?
Pray tell thou me tomorrow.

Traditional rhyme

The Romans named this ancient herb after Achilles, the strong and brave warrior-hero of Homer's *Iliad,* whose spear had the power to heal as well as to kill.

And of Achilles with his queynte spere,
For he coude with it both hele and dere [harm].

Geoffrey Chaucer, *The Squire's Tale*, 1386–1389

Legend says that yarrow grew from the rusty scrapings of Achilles' spear, and it is recorded that Achilles healed many of his wounded fellow warriors in the Trojan War with this herb. Yarrow has been used on the battlefield for its healing qualities throughout history. The Anglo-Saxon name for the herb was *gearwe,* which meant "repairer of bodies," and many Native Americans prized this herb's power to heal cuts and wounds.

In 19th-century Ireland, there was a belief that yarrow was the first herb Jesus picked as a child, and for this reason it was deemed a lucky charm. According to folklore, a person who dreamed of picking yarrow to use as a medicine could shortly expect some good news. The herb was also thought to have the power to heal broken hearts. Wild yarrow is usually white, but there are many colored varieties. It is the birthday flower for January 16th, and symbolizes heartache and cure in the language of flowers. According to the 17th-century herbalist Nicholas Culpeper, it was governed by the planet Venus.

SACRED PROTECTION

Yarrow, sweet yarrow, the first that I have found,
And in the name of Jesus I pluck it from the ground.
As Joseph loved sweet Mary, and took her for his dear,
So in a dream, this night, I hope my true love will appear.

Traditional rhyme

THE DRUIDS ENDOWED THIS HERB WITH sacred powers, and used large stalks of it to divine the weather. The ancient Chinese foretold the future in a ceremony involving yarrow stems, which is described in *The Yarrow Stalk Oracle,* also known as the *I Ching* or *Book of Changes.*

Believed to have potent magical properties, yarrow was assigned to St. John, and was hung in houses and churches on St. John's Eve (June 23rd) to give protection against sickness and evil spirits. Bunches of the herb were nailed to doorways or thrown on a bonfire at sunset. Yarrow was often woven into garlands for decoration in the house and to keep witches and fairies away.

It was thought that witches used the herb in their magic spells and potions, and some common names for yarrow show how the herb was linked with evil spirits, for example: devil's plaything, devil's condiments, and devil's nettle. The latter, however, could have originated from a popular children's game that involved drawing yarrow leaves across the face to create a tingling sensation.

Suspend a bunch of yarrow over the cradle of a newborn baby to keep witches and fairies away.

Hold some yarrow against the eyelids to see whoever is in your thoughts.

FOLKLORE
fever charm

Pull off a yarrow leaf with the left hand while saying the sick person's name. Eat the leaf and the fever in the patient will abate.

HEALTH & HAPPINESS

Plant me a garden to heal the body,
Betony, yarrow and daisies to mend,
Sage for the blood and comfrey for bones
Foxglove and hyssop the sick to tend.

Elizabethan herb song

THIS PLANT WAS SO RESPECTED AS A HEALING herb that it became known as the iodine of the meadows and fields, and it was believed that yarrow grew prolifically in churchyards as a reproach to the dead for not eating yarrow while still alive. In medieval times, yarrow leaves were crushed and used to plug nosebleeds. Conversely, the herb was also used to cause a nosebleed by tickling the internal membranes of the nose with a leaf. The ensuing nosebleed was thought to relieve migraine headaches and lower high blood pressure. Yarrow had such an excellent reputation for lowering fevers that it became known as the fever herb.

Yarrow was traditionally eaten at wedding feasts and included in the bridal bouquet under the name "seven years' love." The herb was thought to ensure that the love between bride and groom would last for at least seven years. In folklore, yarrow was often used as a love oracle. If a woman picked the herb from the grave of a young man on the night of a full moon and placed it under her pillow, she would dream of her future lover.

Test the strength of your lover's feelings by tickling the inside of your nose with a yarrow leaf while saying:
Yarroway, Yarroway, bear a white blow
If my love loves me, my nose will bleed now.

Make a strong infusion of yarrow tea and use the cooled liquid as a mouthwash for inflamed and sore gums.

COLD CURE
brew

1 tsp dried yarrow
1 tsp dried elderflower
½ tsp dried peppermint
Pinch of cayenne pepper

Put the herbs in a warmed pot and pour freshly boiling water over them. Cover and let stand for 10 minutes, then strain. Stir in the cayenne pepper and drink as hot as possible. Add honey to sweeten, if desired.

ANGELICA

Angelica archangelica

Contagious aire ingendering Pestilence
Infects not those that in the mouth have ta'en
Angelica, that happy counterbane
Sent down from Heav'n by some celestial scout
As well the name and nature both avowt.

Guillaume Du Bartas, 16th-century poet

Named after St. Michael the Archangel, angelica was said to flower on his feast day, Michaelmas, on September 29th. Legend tells how the archangel appeared to a monk in a dream and revealed that this magical herb could cure the plague. Another link with the archangel was forged in the 17th century when John Tradescant, an English naturalist, returned home from a trip to Russia with specimens of angelica that he had found growing near the city of Archangel. The 17th-century herbalist John Parkinson thought that the herb was so-named for its heavenly healing virtues, but it is likely that the name came from the Greek *angelos,* meaning "messenger."

All parts of angelica—its bright green leaves, clusters of flower heads, stems, roots, and seeds—were prescribed for many ailments. Angelica was a principal ingredient in a magical rejuvenating elixir thought to prolong life. It acquired a reputation for weaning people from alcohol, was used as a cure for smoking, and was even prescribed to cure the bite of rabid dogs. It was also common practice for concerned parents to mix dried, powdered angelica roots with wine and give the drink to their children in order "to abate the raging lust in young persons"! This herb is the birthday flower for July 11th, and came to symbolize inspiration and gentle melancholy in the ancient language of flowers. According to the 17th-century herbalist Nicholas Culpeper, it is an herb of the sun in Leo.

SACRED PROTECTION

The roote of garden Angelica is a singular remedie against poison, and against the plague, and all infections taken by evil and corrupt aire.

John Gerard, *The Herball or Generall Historie of Plantes*, 1579

THROUGHOUT HISTORY, ANGELICA HAS BEEN credited with magical powers. It was thought to offer protection against witchcraft—no self-respecting witch would use this herb in her magic brews. Angelica was included in many pagan rites because of its renowned purifying qualities. Country folk intoned ancient chants whenever the herb was taken to market, and in some areas, angelica was carried in procession through towns and villages. Angelica was later used in Christian ceremonies and became known as the root of the Holy Ghost. Doctors advised patients to chew angelica to avoid the plague, and the dried roots and seeds were burned in chafing pans over hot coals to disinfect, scent, and purify the home.

Burn the dried roots or seeds to freshen a musty room.

Carry a sprig of angelica to guard against witches' spells.

Air purifier

"Take a root of Angelica, dry it in an oven, or before the fire, then, bruise it well and infuse it 4 or 5 days in white Wine Vinegar. When you use it, lay it upon a brick made red hot, and repeat the operation several times."

***The Toilet of Flora*, 1775**

18TH-CENTURY toilet water

3 handfuls angelica
4 handfuls pennyroyal
4 handfuls rosemary
4 handfuls sage
4 oz (115 g) juniper berries

Choose the freshest herbs you can find, and mix all of the ingredients together in a saucepan. Add a small amount of water and boil for five minutes. Cool and strain the liquid before use.

FLAVOR & FRAGRANCE

In an Iland of the North called Island [Iceland] where it [angelica] groweth very high, it is eaten of the inhabitants ... [and travelers] report that it hath a good and pleasant taste to them that are hungrie.

John Gerard, *The Herball or Generall Historie of Plantes*, 1579

FOR MANY CENTURIES, THE STEMS, LEAVES, AND ROOTS OF ANGELICA WERE HARVESTED IN APRIL and May, then boiled in sugar and candied as sweetmeats. Candied angelica stems were later used for cake decoration. Often the middle ribs of the large leaves were cooked and eaten like asparagus, or the stalks, roots, and stems were dipped in butter and eaten raw. Young leaves or shredded roots were added to salads. The seeds of angelica were used by monks to flavor liqueurs, and this herb was an important ingredient of Eau de Carmes, the famous toilet water invented by the Carmelite monks of Paris.

Wear a garland of angelica to be inspired by its perfume.

Use angelica stalks to save sugar and reduce acidity when cooking fruits such as rhubarb and gooseberries.

After eating garlic, sprinkle the body with angelica water. This will help to reduce the pungency of garlic breath.

CAUTION: Angelica should not be taken internally by diabetics because it increases blood sugar levels.

CANDIED angelica

Use young stems or leaf stalks picked in the spring. Cut into short lengths and put in a saucepan with sufficient water to cover. Simmer until cooked, then drain and remove the outer skin. Return the herb to the saucepan, cover with water, and bring to a boil. Strain and leave the angelica to cool. Weigh the herb and cover with an equal weight of sugar. Leave covered in a cool place for two days. Return the herb, and the syrup that has formed, to a saucepan and simmer gently until the angelica looks fresh and shiny. Strain off the syrup. Sprinkle the angelica liberally with superfine sugar and leave in a cool oven until dry. When cool, wrap in wax paper and store in an airtight container.

GARLIC

Allium sativum

Wel loved he [the repugnant Summoner]
garleek, oynons and eek lekes,
And for to drynken strong wyn, reed as blood.

Geoffrey Chaucer, *The Canterbury Tales*, 1386–1389

GARLIC IS ONE OF THE OLDEST PLANTS KNOWN TO MAN. It is thought to have been used by the early Asian and Indian civilizations, and its name in Sanskrit, the ancient sacred language of Hinduism, intriguingly means "slayer of monsters." This plant was also popular with the ancient Greeks and Romans. According to Greek legend, Odysseus, on his way home from Troy, saved himself and his sailors from the spells of the sorceress Circe by putting a magic plant called moly into the proffered wine. Moly is believed to have been a type of wild garlic. Hecate, the Underworld goddess of magic and charms who was credited with inventing sorcery, was thought to preside over crossroads, and it was traditional to leave garlic there as a votive offering for her supper.

The remarkable healing qualities of this powerfully antiseptic plant endowed it with almost magical properties. People carried garlic cloves to protect themselves from all kinds of evil influences—according to folklore, garlic was capable of repelling vampires. This plant was also used as an aphrodisiac to promote the passions. In some countries, however, garlic was eschewed because of its pungent odor.

The word *garlic* is thought to come from the Anglo-Saxon word *gar* meaning "spear," describing the plant's long, flat leaves, and *leac* or *lac,* Anglo-Saxon for pot herb. According to astrologers, garlic is under the dominion of Mars.

SACRED PROTECTION

If ever a man with impious hand
Strangles an aged parent
May he eat garlic, deadlier than hemlock!

Horace, 1st-century BC poet and satirist

GARLIC WAS THOUGHT TO PROTECT AGAINST witchcraft, evil spirits, and vampire bites during the night. A clove was worn around the neck as a talisman or good luck charm. Sailors carried a clove of garlic whenever they set sail to protect them against shipwreck, and in some areas of France, it was traditional to place a clove of garlic on a child's lips at the baptism ceremony for good health and happiness. Garlic roots were often hung around the necks of blind cattle in the belief that they could restore sight, and German miners carried garlic roots to protect them from the evil spirits that were thought to frequent mines. In Mexico, young girls used garlic to rid themselves of boyfriends whose attentions were no longer welcome.

It was customary to feed game cocks garlic before a fight because it was thought to make them more aggressive, and Roman soldiers ate garlic and carried it into battle to give them added courage. Bullfighters took a clove of garlic into the ring, believing that this would stop the bull from charging. It was thought that to dream of eating garlic signified that hidden secrets were about to be revealed.

● Carry a clove of garlic when at sea to guard against shipwreck. ●

● Wear a necklace of garlic cloves to keep vampires away. ●

● Charm away warts by making three crosses with a garlic clove over them. ●

JAUNDICE protector

Follow this ancient advice to guard against jaundice. Wear a necklace of 13 cloves of garlic for 13 days. On the 13th day, in the middle of the night, go to the junction of two streets, take off the necklace, throw it over your head, and run home without looking back.

HEALING

Eate Leekes in Lide [March] and Ramsins [wild garlic] in May
And all the year after Physitians may play.

Traditional adage

THE ANCIENT EGYPTIANS USED THIS PLANT for its medicinal properties, and an inscription on the Great Pyramid at Giza records the sum of money paid for the garlic cloves, onions, and radishes used to sustain the health and strength of the laborers who built the pyramids. The Greek physician, Galen, christened the plant "heal all" because of its many medicinal properties. Lepers used to peel garlic cloves to eat as a treatment for their condition, and this gave rise to the name "pilgarlic" for a leper in the Middle Ages.

During the plague of Marseilles in 1726, four thieves who were arrested for robbing corpses credited their immunity to the disease to wearing masks soaked in vinegar, garlic, and other herbs. This later became known as "four thieves' vinegar." In the early 19th century, some garlic-eating French priests who were working in the London slums at the height of an infectious fever suffered no adverse health effects, unlike their Anglican non-garlic-eating brethren. The natural antiseptic properties of garlic have always been employed for dressing wounds. During World War I, for example, moss soaked in garlic juice was used as a dressing to prevent wounds from turning septic.

● Mix a finely chopped clove of garlic with 1 tsp grated apple. Eat this slowly as a digestive tonic before going to bed. ●

● Pack a dental cavity with garlic pulp to ease the pain until you can visit a dentist. ●

● Put a clove of garlic in each shoe to treat whooping cough. ●

WONDER tonic

4 whole bulbs of garlic
¾ pint (450 ml) brandy

Marinate the garlic in the brandy for 10 days. Take 1 tbsp in half a glass of water each morning as a general tonic or to treat rheumatism.

A UNIQUE FLAVOR

[The air of Provence is] particularly perfumed by the refined essence of this mystically attractive bulb.

Alexandre Dumas, *Le Grand Dictionnaire de Cuisine*, 1873

GARLIC HAS BEEN POPULAR IN THE KITCHEN THROUGHOUT THE AGES. IT WAS ONE OF THE staple foods of Egyptian peasants, and is depicted on the decorated walls of ancient tombs. The Hebrews, after their flight from Egypt, longed for the garlic that they had grown accustomed to in captivity. The ancient Greeks and Romans used raw garlic in their salads. The Italian explorer Marco Polo, traveling in the Far East in the 13th century, recorded how the poor bought animal livers from slaughterhouses, then chopped up the meat and ate it raw in a garlic sauce.

This plant has acquired a collection of common names through the ages. Many refer pejoratively to its pungent odor, such as onion stinkers, stinking Jenny, and devil's posy. It is recorded that on November 21st, 1368, Alfonso, King of Castile, decreed that any knight who ate garlic be banned from court for 30 days. Many classic dishes, however—such as the Provençal sauce aïoli and the Genoese pesto sauce—rely on garlic for flavoring. During cooking, garlic mellows in flavor and becomes sweeter, so recipes requiring huge amounts of garlic are not the devilish threat you might expect.

GARLIC soup

21 whole bulbs of garlic
4 pints (2.5 liters) water
Bouquet garni of mixed herbs
Salt and black pepper
4 tbsp olive oil
3 oz (75 g) butter
2 oz (50 g) all-purpose flour
2 eggs, beaten

Peel the cloves, then put them in a saucepan with the water, bouquet garni, seasoning, and oil. Bring to a boil and simmer for about one hour. Liquidize until all the cloves are pulped. Melt the butter, stir in the flour, and add to the soup for thickening. Cool slightly before stirring in the beaten eggs. (This soup is especially good for a hangover!)

● Chew cardamom seeds or eat cumin seeds on a green bean to remove the smell of garlic from the breath. ●

● Rub a cut clove of garlic around the dish in which you are serving a salad to impart flavor. ●

TARRAGON

Artemisia dracunculus

For few can resist the charm
Of a sprig of balm
Or the hope of becoming a paragon
By the tactful use of tarragon.

Margaret Brownlow, 20th-century horticulturist and writer

THE GENERIC NAME *ARTEMISIA* IS DERIVED FROM ARTEMIS, THE GREEK FORM OF DIANA, THE ROMAN GODDESS OF THE MOON, HUNTING, AND VIRGINITY. According to legend, Diana gave this group of plants to Chiron, the famous Centaur doctor who lived on Mount Pelion in Thessaly. The word tarragon comes from the French *estragon* and the Arabic *tarkhun,* both meaning "little dragon." It was believed that the plant's long, thin leaves resembled dragons' tongues, and that its coiled, twisted roots were like the curves of a snake's body.

PROTECTION & FLAVOR

[Tarragon] sweetens the breath, dulls the tastes of medicines.

John Gerard, 16th-century apothecary

TARRAGON WAS USED BY THE ROMANS TO ward off exhaustion. The mixed juices of tarragon and fennel were used to make a restorative drink popular with the ancient rulers of India. This plant was thought to cure the bites of snakes and serpents, and to relieve the pain of wasp stings. Tarragon was very popular in Tudor times as a salad plant, and was often eaten before meals to encourage the appetite. When Henry VIII divorced Catherine of Aragon, he is reputed to have cited her reckless use of tarragon as a contributing factor.

Chew the roots of tarragon to ease the pain of toothache.

Put fresh sprigs of tarragon inside your shoes to ward off exhaustion, particularly after standing for long periods.

HERB sandwich

Spread one slice of bread with cream cheese. Chop several sprigs of parsley, chives, marjoram, salad burnet, and tarragon with two leaves of eau-de-Cologne mint and one leaf of sage. Pile the herbs on the cream cheese, top with bread, and serve for a nutritious snack.

CHIVES

Allium schoenoprasum

A salad fit for a King, I sing:
With chives and marjoram, lemon thyme—
A crime to leave out parsley and sprigs of mint—
A hint of sage and bay will crown the head
(in soup or stew) of the newly-wed!

Reginald Arkell, 20th-century poet

Chives were popular with the ancients. The Chinese, who called the herb "jewel among vegetables," used them as culinary and medicinal plants 3000 years before the birth of Christ, and records show that chives were used extensively in Asia and the Mediterranean during pre-Christian times. During his travels in China in the 13th century, Marco Polo was impressed with the culinary versatility of the herb, and when he returned home he enthused about this delicately flavored member of the onion family.

PROTECTION & FLAVOR

Chives next to roses creates posies

Traditional adage

Chives were considered protective plants, and the superstitious would place them around the house to ward off the evil eye. In Chinese folk medicine, chives were used to stop bleeding and as an antidote for poisons. One of the oldest recorded culinary recipes included chives; in 1330 BC, Hu Sihui, the imperial dietician, described how to make a fish salad incorporating the herb. Chive leaves are mildly antibiotic and antiseptic, and this is thought to stimulate the appetite and make fatty foods easier to digest. Chives are mixed with chervil, tarragon, and parsley to make *fines herbes,* the classic blend of mixed herbs used to flavor omelettes, sauces, poultry, and fish.

✣ Make an infusion of chives to spray on gooseberries and cucumber plants to combat mildew. ✣

✣ Plant chives under apple trees to prevent apple scab. ✣

PROTECTIVE posy

Use fresh and dried chive flowers to make a posy, or tussie-mussie. Hang it near a window to keep misfortune away.

Chives are a tasty member of the onion family, with beautiful pale mauve flower heads. This ancient herb is both a visual and culinary delight, and is easy to cultivate.

MINT

Mentha

My lady's fair pew has been strewn full gay
With primroses, cowslips and violets sweet
With mints, with marigolds, and marjorams.

***Appius and Virginia*, 17th-century play variously attributed to John Webster and/or Thomas Heywood**

HADES, GOD OF THE UNDERWORLD, SELDOM VISITED THE WORLD ABOVE, BUT ON ONE TRIP HE FELL IN LOVE WITH THE NYMPH MINTHE. She was dazzled by the splendor of Hades' golden chariot, which was drawn by four magnificent black horses. Hades tried to seduce Minthe, but his wife, Queen Persephone, foiled his plan by changing Minthe into a sweet-smelling plant. Thus, according to legend, the herb mint was created.

Associated with Hecate, the ancient Greek goddess of sorcery and enchantment, mint was a plant much sought by witches for use in their spells and magic brews. The mint pennyroyal was used by witches to make a potion that reputedly caused people who swallowed it to have double vision. Several kinds of mint were included in the Anglo-Saxon magic green salve, which claimed to cure all ills. It was widely believed that anyone finding mint in bloom on St. John's Day (June 24th) would have everlasting happiness. A popular old saying linked mint with more earthly riches:

Grow mint in the garden
to attract money to your purse.

Mint, the birthday flower for February 25th, symbolized burning love, and stood for wisdom and virtue in the ancient floral vocabulary. The 17th-century herbalist Nicholas Culpeper described mint as an herb under the dominion of Venus.

HEALING

If any man can name all the properties of mint,
he must know how many fish swim in the Indian ocean.

Wilafred Strabo, 12th-century poet

MINT WAS CULTIVATED FOR ITS THERAPEUTIC properties by the ancients. Remains of the herb have been discovered in Egyptian tombs dating back to 1000 BC. Herbals written in the 9th and 13th centuries indicate that mint was grown prolifically in monastic gardens. In Tudor times, the herb was made into an antiseptic wash for head sores, and was rubbed on rough tongues. It was mixed with honey and dropped into ears for earache. Women in labor were prescribed powdered mint mixed with wine to ease the pain.

The Greek philosopher Aristotle advised that mint was so powerful an aphrodisiac that people should only take it in moderation, and soldiers were warned to avoid the herb prior to battle lest their courage and vigor be sapped by their increased virility. In *The Thousand and One Nights,* the stories of Sinbad the sailor and Aladdin were recounted by Scheherazade to the Sultan. Scheherazade is reputed to have refreshed herself before sunrise each day by drinking several cups of mint tea.

Aristotle

To cure hiccups, drink the juice of 4 pomegranates with 2–3 chopped sprigs of mint added.

Make peppermint tea to ease indigestion. Use 3 tsp freshly crushed herb per cup of boiling water. Let stand for five minutes before straining and drinking.

MINT foot bath

1 tbsp fresh mint leaves
4 pints (2 liters) boiling water

Cover the mint leaves with the water, let the infusion stand for 15 minutes, then strain. Soak the feet for 20 minutes.

Stomach settler

"Take 2 quarts [4 pints/2 liters] small ale, red mint 2 handfuls, red sage and a little cinnamon. Let it all boil until half be wasted. Sweeten with sugar to your taste and drink night and morning."

Sir Kenelm Digby Bart,
***The Queen's Closet Opened*, 1669**

A FAVORITE SCENT

But those which Perfume the Aire most delightfully, not passed by as the rest, but being troden upon and Crushed, are Three: That is Burnet, Wilde-Time, and Water-Mints.

Francis Bacon, *An Essay of Gardens*, 1625

MINT WAS A FAVORITE SCENT OF THE ANCIENT Greeks and Romans. They wove crowns of the herb to bedeck themselves and their guests at feasts, and put bunches of mint on the table and strewed the plant on floors. It was customary for brides to wear a mint crown or *corona Veneris* as a symbol of good luck. The Greeks rubbed their arms with mint to give them strength, and added it to their bathwater and made sweet-smelling toilet water from the aromatic leaves. Throughout the centuries, country folk filled pomanders with mint leaves, believing that the fragrant aroma refreshed a tired mind. During Georgian times, men carried the dried, powdered leaves of the herb in small silver boxes and inhaled a pinch of this snuff to revive themselves when necessary.

According to folklore, mint helped to repel insects. It was a popular strewing herb in medieval times, and would often be found in butcher's shops and wherever meat was stored to keep flies away. Mint was the main ingredient in early mouthwashes and toothpastes.

SWEET SLEEP sweet bag

"Take drie Rose leaves, keep them close in a glasse which will keep them sweet, then take powder of Mints, powder of Cloves ... and put the same to the Rose leaves, then put all these together in a bag, and take that to bed with you, and it will cause you to sleep, and it is good to smell unto at other times."

Ram's *Little Dodoen*, 1606

Chew a paste of mint and honey to sweeten the breath after drinking alcohol.

Wear a wreath of mint to refresh you when feeling tired.

Rub mint on hives to attract bees.

Storing fresh mint

Wash the herb under cold, running water. Shake it well, place it in a screw-top glass jar, and turn the jar upside down.

CHERVIL

Anthriscus cerefolium

Chervil is handsom and proper
for the edging of kitchin Garden beds.

John Evelyn, 17th-century diarist

CHERVIL WAS BELIEVED TO BE ONE OF THE WARMING SPICES USED TO MAKE THE OIL WITH WHICH MOSES BLESSED THE VESSELS OF THE TABERNACLE. It was one of the magical herbs used by witches when preparing their potions and ointments, because it was believed that its concentrated juice made people see double. The botanical name is thought to be derived from the Greek for "leaves of joy" or "rejoicing in its leaves." In the language of flowers, chervil stands for sincerity, and according to ancient herbalists, it is under the dominion of Jupiter.

PROTECTION & FLAVOR

It is good for old people—it rejoiceth and comforteth the heart and increaseth their strength.

John Gerard, 16th-century apothecary

CHERVIL WAS A VALUABLE MEDICINAL PLANT in the Middle Ages. It was used as an eyewash or compress to treat inflamed eyes and wrinkles around the eyes. It was used in the treatment of blood clots, and women in labor were bathed in it. Chervil was frequently used in sauces designed to make Lenten food more appetizing. It was one of the first herbs available each spring in large quantities, and was served as a soup or broth to revitalize the blood after the long winter months. Chervil is an ingredient in the classic mixture of *fines herbes,* essential to French cuisine.

Chew chervil leaves to cure hiccups.

Squeeze the juice from chervil leaves onto a sting to alleviate the pain.

WRINKLE softener

Soak a cloth in an infusion of chervil leaves and apply it to the affected area.

CHAMOMILE

Chamaemelum nobile

... large walks, broad and long, like the Temple groves
in Thessaly, raised with gravel and sand,
having seats and banks of Chamomile—
all this delights the mind and brings health to the body.

William Lawson, 17th-century writer

THE ANCIENT EGYPTIANS REVERED THIS HERB, AND DEDICATED IT TO THEIR GODS AND TO THE SUN. The Anglo-Saxons called chamomile *maythen*, and chose it as one of their nine sacred herbs in the *Lacnunga,* an early Anglo-Saxon manuscript. According to German legend, chamomile flowers represented the souls of ill-fated soldiers, who for their sins died under a curse. This herb is associated with St. John, and on his day (June 24th) it was customary to hang a chamomile wreath on the door of a house to give protection against thunder, lightning, and storms.

On Midsummer Eve or Midsummer Day (June 23rd or 24th), people lit bonfires at crossroads and in fields. The bonfires were fueled with aromatic plants, including chamomile, that gave off a thick smoke. The smoke was believed to have magical powers that could remove all misfortune. People jumped over the fires, sometimes seven times, drove the pungent smoke toward crops, orchards, and animals, and brought their sick to inhale its beneficial properties.

In many European countries, rural folk took a *bouquet d'église,* a small posy of seasonal flowers, whenever they went to church. Chamomile was the flower used for celebrations on the feast day of St. Anne (July 26th). In south Wales, this herb was one of the sweet-scented flowers traditionally planted on family graves. Chamomile is the birthday flower for December 17th. In the language of flowers, this herb stands for energy in adversity, and in Tudor England it symbolized humility and patience. According to the 17th-century herbalist Nicholas Culpeper, chamomile is an herb of the sun.

HEALING

The anthemis [chamomile] a small but glorious flower
Scarce rears his head, yet has a giant's tower:
Forces the lurking fever to retreat …

Abraham Cowley, 17th-century writer

CHAMOMILE HAS BEEN A MAJOR HEALING herb in folk medicine throughout the centuries. In ancient Egypt, the priests who devoted their lives to tending the sick in the House of Life, the building adjoining most major temples, considered chamomile to be a sacred healing herb. They used it to treat many ailments, including the ague, fevers, colds, most aches and pains, and female disorders.

The ancient Romans believed that chamomile was an antidote to the poisonous bites of serpents. Long-used for its calming and sedative properties, chamomile tea was prescribed for hysteria, sleep problems, digestive troubles, depression, and delirium tremens. In the late 19th century, this herb was used as a quinine-substitute for the treatment of malaria, and it was thought beneficial for consumptives (those suffering from tuberculosis) to sit near chamomile beds to breathe in the herb's scent. Dried chamomile leaves were smoked or taken as snuff to treat asthma and insomnia. When the herb was first introduced into North America, it was used as a poultice on wounds to prevent gangrene.

❀ Make a strong infusion of chamomile tea. Add it to your bathwater to reduce muscle fatigue. This also helps to ease the symptoms of cystitis and thrush. ❀

❀ Use strained, cooled chamomile tea to bathe a sty around the eye. ❀

❀ Steep some chamomile teabags in a bowl of boiling water and inhale the vapor to alleviate hayfever or a stuffy nose. ❀

EYE sparkler

2–3 tbsp chamomile flowers
1 pint (600 ml) boiling water

Cover the flowers with the boiling water and let it infuse. Cool, then pour the solution into an ice-cube tray and freeze. Remove a chamomile cube whenever you have tired eyes, and rub it gently around the eye sockets, over the eyelids, and over the eyebrows.

COMFORT

Plant me a garden to heal the heart,
Balm for joy, and the sweet violet
Cowslips, pansies and chamomile
To ease the pain I want to forget.

Elizabethan herb song

IN ADDITION TO BEING A POPULAR FRAGRANT strewing herb around the house and at wedding celebrations, chamomile was also boiled with orange peel to make scented washing water. Chamomile was used for lightening and brightening the hair, and was a favorite flower to include in herb bouquets, or tussie-mussies. In England, for example, it has been customary for centuries to carry herbal posies at coronations, and when Elizabeth II was crowned in 1953, she was handed a tussie-mussie containing chamomile.

Often grown on banks and in raised beds in old herb gardens to delight the senses, this herb was also made into carpet walks and lawns. The country name, herb of humility, refers to the plant's ability to thrive when walked on. It is said that Sir Francis Drake was enjoying his customary game of bowls at Plymouth on a chamomile lawn when the Spanish Armada was sighted in the English Channel in 1588. This herb was an ingredient of herb beer, and in the 19th century, it was used in a popular tonic called chamomile bitters.

❀ Make a posy, or tussie-mussie, of chamomile flowers flanking a sprig of sage to give to an aged relative or friend. In the language of flowers, this arrangement stands for wisdom and the serenity of years. ❀

❀ Sit near a bed of chamomile and breathe in its strength-giving scent. ❀

COMFORTING skin cleanser

2–3 tbsp chamomile flowers
1 pint (600 ml) water
1 tsp lemon juice

Put the flowers and water in a saucepan and simmer for 10 minutes. Cool and strain the liquid. Add the lemon juice and store in the refrigerator in a sealed container. When needed, gently cleanse the face and neck with the lotion using a soft cotton pad.

"Flore Pleno" is a beautiful variety of chamomile, with sumptuous, sweet-smelling flowers. This healing and cosmetic herb of antiquity is a feast for all the senses.

FENNEL

Foeniculum vulgare

Above the lowly plants it towers,
The fennel, with its yellow flowers ...

Henry Wadsworth Longfellow, *The Goblet of Life*, 19th century

Legend linked this herb with Adonis, the beautiful Greek child beloved by Aphrodite who was fatally wounded by a wild boar. The grieving Aphrodite ordered that fennel should be used at the funeral rites, presumably because the plant grows quickly and then fades and dies suddenly, mirroring the fate of Adonis. Fennel also appears in the story of Prometheus, who stole fire from the gods to give to mankind, and escaped from Olympus carrying a burning ember in the hollow stalk of a giant fennel plant.

This herb was much prized for its medicinal properties. The ancients believed that fennel was excellent for the eyes. Pliny declared that it cleared the eyes to appreciate the beauty of nature, and could help people to see when their sight had been impaired. Greek athletes and warriors thought the herb gave them added stamina and strength. Roman gladiators included fennel in their diet as a stimulant, and at the end of gladiatorial contests, the victors were bedecked with a fennel garland.

It gave men strength and fearless mood,
And gladiators fierce and rude
Mingled it in their daily food;
And he who battled and subdued,
The wreath of Fennel wore.

Henry Wadsworth Longfellow, *The Goblet of Life*, 19th century

Fennel stands for merit in the ancient floral vocabulary. It is the birthday flower for December 5th, and according to the 17th-century herbalist Nicholas Culpeper, is an herb of Mercury under Virgo.

SACRED PROTECTION

On the vigil of St. John Baptist every man's door being shadowed with green birch, long fennel ... and suchlike, ... had also lamps of glass, with oil burning in them all the night ... which made a goodly show.

John Stow, *Survey of London*, 1598

Fennel was dedicated to St. John, and on his feast day on June 24th, bunches of the herb were hung over doorways and windows as a charm against evil spirits entering during the year. It was one of the nine sacred herbs that the ancients used as a preventative against evil influences. Fennel seeds were placed in the keyholes of haunted houses in the belief that they would keep ghosts away. Fennel was thought to be able to restore sexual powers, and was included in medieval love potions. It was one of the herbs strewn in the pathways of newlyweds.

Magical chant

Intone this ancient chant when taking herbal potions to increase their efficacy:

Thyme and fennel,
a pair great in power,
The Wise Lord, holy in heaven,
Wrought these herbs
while he hung on the cross;
He placed and put them
in the seven worlds
To aid all, poor and rich.

TO CONJURE demons

The smoke from this ancient recipe was reputed to produce demons. Burn together fennel, coriander, parsley, hemlock, liquor of black poppy, sandalwood, and henbane.

Put fennel seeds in keyholes to keep malignant forces away.

Soak fennel seeds in wine, then drink the wine to revitalize your love life.

Bathe the eyes of a newborn baby with fennel water to improve its eyesight.

FLAVOR & FRAGRANCE

A savoury odour blown
Grateful to appetite, more pleased my sense
Than smell of sweetest Fennel.

John Milton, *Paradise Lost*, 1667–1674

ALL PARTS OF THIS FRAGRANT HERB HAVE BEEN USED IN COOKERY. THE FEATHERY LEAVES WERE put under loaves of bread to add flavor, and the aromatic seeds were sprinkled on top. The roots and stems were cooked and eaten as a vegetable, and the leaves and seeds were added to salads, sauces, fish dishes, and preserves. It is known that the Emperor Charlemagne loved the herb and encouraged its cultivation on his imperial farms, and it is recorded that crops of fennel grew profusely in the Spanish countryside during the 10th century. It was common practice for the poor to eat fennel to dull the appetite and stave off hunger pangs. The Puritans who settled in the New World chewed fennel seeds in church, as well as dill seeds, to still their hunger during long, tedious sermons. Both herbs became known as Meetin' House seeds.

Fennel was also a popular strewing herb. Its leaves were sweet-smelling and an effective flea-repellent. When the Portuguese first discovered the island of Madeira, they were struck by the overpowering fragrance of the wild fennel growing there. They called the place where they landed Funchal, from the Portuguese word *funcho,* meaning fennel.

FENNEL sauce

"Pick green fennel, mint and parsley, a little of each; wash them clean, and boil them till tender, drain and press them, chop them fine, add melted butter, and serve up the sauce immediately, for if the herbs are mixed any length of time before it is served up to table they will be discoloured. If approved, there may be added the pulp of green gooseberries rubbed through a hair sieve, and a little sifted sugar."

Richard Dolby, *Cook's Dictionary and Housekeeper's Directory*, 1832

Carry some fennel seeds in an airtight container to use as smelling salts.

Cook a whole fish on a fragrant bed of fennel leaves to impart flavor.

WORMWOOD

Artemisia absinthium

… these for frenzy be
A speedy and a sovereign remedy,
The bitter wormwood, sage and marigold;
Such sympathy with man's good they do hold

John Fletcher, *The Faithful Shepherdess*, c. 1610

Wormwood is linked with the Greek goddess of chastity, Artemis, who took care of women during childbirth and is said to have made much use of this herb. The Greeks believed that when added to wine, the herb made it less intoxicating. Legend has it that when the serpent was expelled from the Garden of Eden, wormwood sprang up along the tracks it made. This herb stands for absence and displeasure in the language of flowers. The birthday flower for April 29th, wormwood was thought to be an herb of Mars.

SACRED PROTECTION

Where chamber is sweeped and wormwood is strewn,
no flea for his life, dare abide to be knowne.

Thomas Tusser, 16th-century writer

According to Pliny, branches of wormwood were carried in procession by Egyptian priests who worshipped Isis, goddess of magic. From medieval times onward, country folk hung wormwood near doorways to give protection from evil spirits and vampires. A wormwood salve was rubbed on the skin of those suffering from nocturnal visitors. It was believed that witches added this herb to their potions for its hallucinogenic effect, and to induce an increased state of susceptibility in their clients. In household folklore, wormwood was an important disinfectant.

❖ Rub an infusion of wormwood and rosemary on the scalp each night and morning to cure baldness. ❖

INSECT repellent

Put equal quantities of dried wormwood, lavender, and mint into small cheesecloth bags and hang wherever required.

RUE

Ruta graveolens

A weary lot is thine, fair maid,
A weary lot is thine!
To pull the thorn thy brow to braid,
And press the rue for wine!

Sir Walter Scott, *Rokeby*, 1813

THE NAME OF THIS HERB IS DERIVED FROM THE LATIN *RUTA,* MEANING "BITTERNESS" OR "UNPLEASANTNESS," AND THE GREEK *REUO,* WHICH MEANS "TO SET FREE," PRESUMABLY BECAUSE THE HERB WAS THOUGHT TO BE EFFECTIVE IN TREATING SO MANY AILMENTS. However, the common names, herb of repentance and herb of grace, come from the custom of sprinkling holy water from branches of rue before the Catholic celebrations of High Mass. The herb, therefore, became synonymous with the grace that followed repentance.

There's rue for you, and here's some for me
We may call it herb of grace o' Sundays.

William Shakespeare, *Hamlet*, 1602

Rue is one of the few herbs used in heraldry. In 1181, the Emperor Barbarossa decreed that the first Duke of Saxony could include a wreath of rue on his coat of arms, and 600 years later the Order of the Crown of Rue was created by the first king of Saxony. This herb is also featured in the Collar of the Order of the Thistle. The small, rounded, lobed leaves of rue are supposed to have inspired the design of the suit of clubs in the deck of playing cards. Rue is the birthday flower for January 18th, and in the ancient floral vocabulary stands for fecundity in the fields.

SACRED PROTECTION

First they are to try the devil
by holy water, incense, sulphur, rue,
which from thence, as we suppose,
came to be called "herb of grace".

Jeremy Taylor, *A Dissuasive from Popery*, 1664

THROUGHOUT HISTORY, PEOPLE HAVE VENERATED THIS HERB. It was thought to give protection against witchcraft, spells, curses, and the evil eye. Rue was grown by innkeepers so that travelers could be given some to keep them safe on their journey. In the Tyrol, it was traditional to bind together rue, broom, maidenhair, agrimony, and ground ivy. Anyone carrying such a posy was protected from evil and would be able to detect witches. Throughout the Christian and Islamic world, rue was thought to have the power to exorcise the devil.

Throughout the ages, rue has been associated with misfortune, and this gave rise to today's expression "you will rue the day." In olden days, people who felt aggrieved would throw a bunch of rue at the person who had wronged them, while uttering the curse "may you rue this day as long as you live." The dried leaves of rue were thought to be a powerful germ killer, and it was considered the most potent of the disinfectant strewing herbs. According to folklore, rue was said to have the ability to make ammunition more deadly, and musket balls and gun flints were soaked or boiled in rue and vervain water so that they would hit their target every time.

MEDIEVAL madness cure

Collect some dew at midnight and mix it with rue to cure madness:

"sprinkled she the juice of Rue
With nine drops of the
midnight dew."

Michael Drayton, 16th–17th-century poet

✿ Rub the floor of your house with rue to expel witches. ✿

✿ Plant the herb in window boxes to create a screen against misfortune. ✿

HEALING

What savour is better, if Physicke be true
For places infected, than wormwood and rue.

Thomas Tusser, 16th-century writer

The Greeks and Romans venerated this herb for its medicinal properties. They believed that rue protected the eyesight, and even had the power to confer second sight. Pliny described how craftsmen such as engravers, printers, and wood carvers took drafts of rue to relieve eyestrain, and both Leonardo da Vinci and Michelangelo claimed that the herb's metaphysical powers had improved their creative vision. Medieval monks working on illuminated manuscripts took rue to ease their headaches, and the herb was also made into a soothing eye salve. The Greek physician Dioscorides praised this herb as being good for coughs and inflammations, and it was also used to treat stomach upsets, muscular cramps, nervous complaints, and high blood pressure.

Country folk thought that rue was safe to use medicinally if it was gathered in the morning, but if picked later in the day, the herb was deemed poisonous. It was said to be more potent when grown under a fig tree, and curiously was considered better if stolen from a neighbor's garden. Bite wounds from a rabid dog were encased in rue leaves. The herb, steeped in wine and drunk, was thought to ease scorpion, bee, and wasp stings as well as snake bites.

✿ Suspend rue around your neck and simultaneously renounce the devil and all his works to ease attacks of vertigo. ✿

✿ Rinse rue in vinegar and lay it on your forehead to improve the memory. ✿

✿ Plug the nose with rue leaves to staunch a nosebleed. ✿

ANCIENT fever cure

When the moon is on the wane, take a handful of dandelion, agrimony, verjuice, rue, powdered crabs' eyes and claws, and yarrow from a grave. Boil together for some hours. In ancient times, drinking this potion was reputed to cure fevers.

BORAGE

Borago officinalis

When talking of borage this much is clear
That it warms the heart and it brings good cheer.

Advice from the 11th-century medical school of Salerno, Italy

THERE IS SOME DISPUTE ABOUT THE ORIGIN OF THIS HERB'S NAME. Some think it may be derived from the Latin word *burra,* meaning a coarse cloth or hairy garment, in which case it probably describes the rough, bristly texture of borage leaves. However, others have suggested that the name is a corruption of *corago*—*cor* (heart) and *ago* (I bring)—and indicates that borage had a reputation as a tonic and cheering cordial. Pliny called borage *euphrosynum,* because it made people cheerful and happy, and its Welsh name is translated as "herb of gladness." It is thought that borage was the herb called *nepenthe* by the Greek epic poet Homer. According to legend, it induced complete amnesia or forgetfulness when added to wine.

Used extensively by the Romans, this herb was probably spread throughout Europe by them. Early European settlers took borage to North America, where, according to a record dated 1631, it was called *burradge.* This beautiful herb has been a popular motif in needlework designs for many centuries, and it is said that its cobalt-blue flowers inspired artists when painting the blue robes worn by the Virgin Mary. Louis XIV of France loved this herb so much that he had it planted in the gardens of his palace at Versailles. In the language of flowers, borage stands for bluntness, courage, and cheerfulness, and it was described as an herb of Jupiter under Leo by early astrologers.

CAUTION: Borage is a scheduled herb in Australia and New Zealand, where it can be used externally but not internally. Borage is available in the United States and Britain for both internal and external use.

PROTECTION & HEALING

Borage and Hellebore fill two scenes,
Sovereign plants to purge the veins
Of melancholy, and cheer the heart
Of those black fumes which make it smart.

Robert Burton, *The Anatomy of Melancholy*, 1621

IN FOLK LEGEND, BORAGE WAS THOUGHT OF as a protective plant, and was linked with courage from the days of the ancient Greeks. This is illustrated by the custom of floating borage in the farewell stirrup cup offered to knights setting off on hazardous crusades. Similarly, in medieval England, a borage infusion was drunk by contestants before fighting in jousting tournaments to make them feel brave.

COSMETIC bath

"Take 2 lb [1 kg] of Barley or Bean-meal, 8 lb [3.5 kg] of Bran, and a few handfuls of Borage leaves. Boil these ingredients in a sufficient quantity of spring water. Nothing cleanses and softens the skin like this bath."

***The Toilet of Flora*, 1775**

In popular medicine, the seeds, leaves, flowers, and roots of this herb were all put to good use. The young leaves were used to make green tea, an herbal infusion that acted as a tonic or cheering cordial, and was also prescribed to induce sweating and reduce fevers. More recently, it was customary to give borage tea to young ladies who were lovesick—the herb was thought to cure the swooning palpitations of the heart and ease the pangs of unrequited love. In the Middle Ages, it was customary for wet nurses to drink soups flavored with borage in the belief that the herb ensured a good supply of milk.

★ Make an infusion of borage leaves. When cool, strain the liquid and soak a clean cloth in it. Wring out the cloth and apply it as a cooling compress to ease tired legs after standing for a long time. ★

★ Pour boiling water over borage leaves, and using a towel to enclose the steam, inhale the vapor to treat dry facial skin. After 10 minutes, rinse the face in tepid water, pat dry, and apply a moisturizer. ★

FLAVOR & FRAGRANCE

A jug of homemade lemonade with a sprig of borage floating at the top circulated at the upper end of the table.

Flora Thompson, *Lark Rise to Candleford* (describing a hay-home supper), 1945

Borage has been a useful herb in the kitchen throughout the centuries. The leaves were chopped and added to salads, or cooked like spinach as a vegetable, and it was considered a valuable pot herb to add to soups, stews, and casseroles. In Elizabethan times, it was traditional to cook borage with mutton. A traditional plowman's lunch in the 18th century consisted of bread, cheese, cider, and a few borage leaves. Borage flowers and leaves have a cucumber-like flavor, which made the herb a popular addition to wine cups. This is illustrated in some of the herb's common names, such as cool tankard and herb of gladness.

The practice of making and giving gifts of sweet waters for special days, such as birthdays, was popular at the time of the Tudors and Stuarts. In 1502, the household record of the Earl of Northumberland listed borage as one of the herbs used for making sweet water. For dessert, borage flowers were crystalized or coated in sugar syrup, and according to one 16th-century recipe, borage-flavored egg custards were popular.

★ Plant borage in your garden to attract bees, butterflies, and hummingbirds. ★

★ Put the flowers carefully in ice-cube trays and cover with water. Freeze. Float the ice-cubed flowers in fruit drinks and wine for decoration. ★

CANDIED borage flowers

Choose perfect flowers and gently pull each blossom off the plant by its black center. Wash carefully and set on a paper towel to dry. Using a fine brush, paint each flower with egg white and dust with superfine sugar until completely coated. Spread some wax paper on a tray and sprinkle with superfine sugar. Transfer the borage flowers onto the tray. Leave for 24 hours in a warm, dry place (but not in the sun). When dry, store in an airtight container between layers of wax paper. Use as a garnish for cake and ice cream.

DILL

Anethum graveolens

Therewith her vervain and dill
That hindreth witches of their will

Michael Drayton, 16th-century poet

DILL WAS TRADITIONALLY BELIEVED TO HAVE PROTECTIVE POWERS, AND WAS USED TO COUNTERACT THE SPELLS AND CURSES OF WITCHES AND SORCERERS. This aromatically sweet herb, first recorded some 5000 years ago in an Egyptian doctor's list of remedies, was known and used by ancient civilizations for its medicinal properties. The ancient Egyptians employed it to treat headaches, and the Romans and Greeks grew it in their gardens to use as both a food and a perfumed incense, as well as for its therapeutic qualities. Both Pliny and Dioscorides wrote of its calming powers and called the herb *anethon.* It was cultivated in Palestine and is widely believed to be the anise mentioned in the Bible.

Woe unto you, scribes and Pharisees, hypocrites!
for ye pay tithe of mint and anise and cummin,
and have omitted the weightier matters of the law.

The Bible, St. Matthew XXIII:23

The Romans took the plant to Britain, where it was used extensively. At the time of Queen Boudicea's rebellion in Roman Britain, a shop in Colchester that sold herbs was burned down. Recent excavations at the site have uncovered burned dill seeds, along with aniseeds, coriander seeds, celery seeds, and poppy seeds. Dill grew wild in Britain in Saxon times, and its name is derived from the Anglo-Saxon *dylle* and the old Norse *dilla,* both meaning "to lull." Ancient herbalists assigned this herb to the domination of Mercury.

SACRED PROTECTION

[Use dill to] strengthen the brain,
[it] stayeth the belly ...
and is a gallant expeller of wind.

Nicholas Culpeper, *The English Physician*, c. 1653

In Anglo-Saxon times, dill was a major ingredient of a cure-all magic holy salve. It was used in a charm purporting to rid sufferers of water-elf disease (thought to be chicken pox), and was also used to treat elf disease (probably jaundice). Many glowing descriptions of the herb's magical powers appear in the diaries of Alfric, Archbishop of Canterbury in 10th-century England.

Dill was thought to have protective powers against the charms and curses of witches and sorcerers. Paradoxically, it was also thought to be one of the herbs used by magicians in their spells. Dill was considered an aphrodisiac and was infused in wine to enhance passion. It was also a constituent of love potions and charms. Throughout history, this herb has been used to soothe restless children. Women would rub their breasts with dill juice to lull suckling babies to sleep after feeding. Even today, dill is one of the main ingredients in gripe water, used to calm a fretful infant. Throughout history, dill has been used to treat indigestion and stomach upsets.

CHILD calmer

Infuse ½ tsp dill in a cup of boiling water for five minutes. Strain, cool, and give the child sips from a teaspoon.

Chew dill seeds to promote healthy digestion and freshen the breath.

Make a protective potion by boiling together equal amounts of dill, trefoil, St. John's wort, and vervain. Place the infusion by the main entrance to your house to prevent bad luck from entering.

Brew dill tea to treat insomnia.

FLAVOR & FRAGRANCE

To keep greene cucumbers all the yeare,
cut the cucumbers in peeces,
boyle them in spring-water, sugar, and dill, a walnut or two:
take them up and let your pickle stand untill it be cold.

Jane Mosley, 17th-century housewife

DILL WAS AN INVALUABLE HERB IN EARLY Greece, and was also known to the ancient Romans, who grew it in their gardens for use as a food flavoring. It was a common and popular pot herb in medieval times. All parts of the plant were used for seasoning, and the herb was added to salads and used for preserving vegetables for the winter. The Greeks and Romans used dill oil for perfumed incense. Among other cosmetic preparations, dill was used to strengthen the fingernails.

Often called false fennel because of its similarity to this plant, dill was one of the precious seeds taken to the New World by the early settlers from Europe. It is recorded that a John Winthrop cultivated the herb there in the 17th century. Around this time, it was popular to eat dill seeds during long church services. They have a mildly soporific effect and can relieve the pangs of hunger, so presumably the congregations found them helpful during long and tedious sermons. This custom explains one of the herb's more curious common names, House seeds or Meetin' House seeds.

Use ground dill seed to season food as an alternative to salt. This herb is especially useful in a salt-free diet.

Add chopped dill leaves to pickles, green vegetables, cucumber salads, and fish sauces.

Strengthen your fingernails by regularly soaking them for 10 minutes in a strong infusion of dill seeds.

DILL vinegar

2 tbsp dill seeds
1 pint (600 ml) white wine vinegar

Put the dill seeds in a sterile glass bottle. Add the vinegar and seal the bottle tightly. Store in the dark for 2–3 weeks, then strain into another sterile bottle. Use in salad dressings, mayonnaise, and other sauces.

venerable
aromatic
LOVE &
stimulating
soothing
fortifying

DEATH

Most of the love potions and charms of ancient folklore have contained **herbs** as their most important ingredient. Some **herbs** were used to make fragrant posies and were presented by lovers to the object of their affection. **Herbs** were worn at weddings and were important inclusions in bridal bouquets. Certain **herbs**, however, were linked with death and the process of dying. They were featured in funeral rites and were used to adorn coffins, funeral processions, graves, and wayside shrines. In many cultures, **herbal** oils were applied during the process of embalming.

ROSEMARY

Rosmarinus officinalis

Rosemary is for remembrance
Between us day and night
Wishing I may always
Have you in my sight.

Traditional rhyme

THE ANCIENT ROMANS ADORNED THEIR HOUSEHOLD GODS WITH ROSEMARY, AND PURIFIED THEIR FLOCKS IN THE SMOKE FROM THE BURNING HERB. In ancient Greece, scholars entwined it in their hair and massaged rosemary oil into their foreheads to strengthen the memory. Early Arab physicians revered the herb and thought it could restore lost vitality, memory, and speech.

Legend links the name of this herb with the Virgin Mary. It was believed that rosemary flowers were originally white, but that Mary, on her flight to Egypt after the birth of Jesus, threw her blue cloak over a rosemary bush while she rested. When she removed it, the white flowers had turned a lovely blue in her honor, and have remained that color ever since. It is said that the shrub only grows as tall as the height of Christ, and that after 33 years, the age at which Christ was crucified, rosemary either stops growing or withers away. Believed to thrive only for the virtuous, rosemary was considered a symbol of the Nativity of Christ. It was thought to be one of the two herbs taken by Adam and Eve when they were expelled from the Garden of Eden; for this reason, God gave it special health-giving powers to comfort mankind.

The name rosemary is derived from the Latin *Ros-marinus,* meaning "dew of the sea," because the herb thrives in coastal regions. In the language of flowers, rosemary means "your presence revives me," and in the ancient floral vocabulary it stands for remembrance. This herb is the birthday flower for January 17th, and according to astrologers, it is an herb of the sun.

LOVE & DEATH

Grow it for two ends, it matters not at all,
Be't for my bridal or my burial.

Robert Herrick, 17th-century poet

ROSEMARY HAS LONG BEEN ASSOCIATED WITH BOTH WEDDINGS AND FUNERALS. IT WAS traditional to dip sprigs of the herb in scented water for the groom and bridesmaids to carry at a wedding ceremony. The bride wore a wreath of the herb, or inserted sprigs of it into her bouquet. If cuttings of rosemary from the bouquet were then planted in the bridal couple's garden and took root, this signified that the woman would be master of the house. Throughout history, rosemary has been used as a love oracle, and if a girl placed a silver coin and a sprig of rosemary under her pillow, she would dream of a future lover.

Rosemary represented faithful remembrance, so it was universally used at funeral services, and was often referred to as the funeral flower. Sprigs of the herb were distributed to mourners, who then threw the sprigs onto the nailed coffin. In some countries, it was traditional to put the herb in the hands of the dead.

⁜ Put a bowl of flour under a rosemary bush on Midsummer's Eve (June 23rd). In the morning, the initials of a future spouse will be traced in the flour. ⁜

⁜ Gild sprigs of rosemary, then tie them together with a gold ribbon. Present them as favors to wedding guests. ⁜

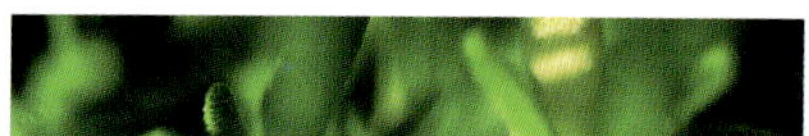

TO DREAM of love

1 tsp wine
1 tsp rum
1 tsp vinegar
1 tsp water
Sprig of rosemary

Mix all of the liquid ingredients in a glass bottle. Dip the sprig of rosemary into it and pin the herb to your breast on St. Magdalen's Eve (July 21st). This will allow you to have prophetic dreams of a future lover.

HEALING & COMFORT

... rosemary, the flowers of which are credibly reported to give their scent about thirty leagues off at sea upon the coasts of Spain.

John Evelyn, 17th-century diarist

ROSEMARY WAS ONCE REGARDED AS A PLANT that could cure all ills. It was made into a tonic tea to stimulate the entire body, and leaves of the herb were added to wine to strengthen the heart. This herb was also used to ease coughs and colds. Rosemary was often burned in the sickroom because of its antiseptic qualities, and was used in recipes to prevent the plague. In times of an epidemic, fresh rosemary was carried in neck pouches and sniffed continually. As recently as Victorian times, the herb was carried in the hollowed handles of walking sticks for its protective properties. A poultice of boiled rosemary leaves was prescribed to treat gout.

In the 13th century, Queen Elizabeth of Hungary was a firm advocate of a toilet water distilled from rosemary flowers and white wine, which was reputed to be responsible for her youthful appearance. The French believed that rosemary flowers had the power to rekindle lost energy, and one ancient Italian recipe used the flowers of rosemary, rue, sage, marjoram, fennel, and quince to make a potion to preserve youth. It was customary for rural folk to spread their laundry on rosemary bushes to dry, so that the damp linen absorbed the fragrance of the herb.

⁜ Crush rosemary flowers and bind them to your right arm to make you feel light and merry. ⁜

⁜ Wash your face in a decoction of rosemary and white wine to preserve youthful looks. ⁜

⁜ Massage the scalp with oil of rosemary to cure baldness. ⁜

HEADACHE reliever

6 drops rosemary essential oil
1 pint (600 ml) cold water

Stir the oil into the water and soak a soft cloth in the bowl for a few minutes. Wring out the cloth and apply it as a cold compress to your forehead, pressing down lightly with your fingertips. Lie back and relax for a minute, then remove the cloth. Relax for another minute while you resoak the compress, then repeat the process several times.

FLAVOR & FRAGRANCE

A few slices of bread and home-made lard, flavoured with rosemary ... "went down good" as they used to say.

Flora Thompson, *Lark Rise to Candleford* (describing a hay-home supper), 1945

ROSEMARY HAS BEEN A POPULAR CULINARY HERB THROUGHOUT THE AGES. ITS AROMATIC SMELL gave flavor to meat, fish, and vegetables. The flowers were added to salads, preserved in wine and vinegar, or candied in a sugar syrup. It was used in the brewing of beer, where its pungency was thought to offset the sweetness of the malt. The Welsh believed that cooking spoons carved from rosemary wood made food more nutritious, and it was common practice to drink from a rosemary spoon in the belief that this afforded protection from poison. The main course of the Christmas feast was often a roasted boar's head decorated with rosemary, which was ceremonially carried to the dining table. In Elizabethan England, it was traditional to present sprigs of scented rosemary to guests on New Year's Day, together with an orange decorated with cloves.

ROSEMARY scones

8 oz (225 g) self-rising flour
2 oz (50 g) butter
1 oz (25 g) superfine sugar
1 tbsp finely chopped rosemary leaves
1 beaten egg
A little milk

Rub the butter into the flour, then stir in the sugar and rosemary. Add the egg and milk and mix until it forms a soft dough. Knead lightly and roll out on a floured board until ¾ in (2 cm) thick. Cut out circles of dough, and place them on a baking tray. Brush the tops with milk. Bake in the oven at 425°F (220°C/gas mark 7) for 10–12 minutes. Split the scones in half, spread with butter, and eat while still hot.

⁂ Press sprigs of rosemary between the pages of books so that its fragrance will perfume the paper. ⁂

⁂ Add a sprig of rosemary to wine and fruit drinks for an unusual flavor. ⁂

Sleep tight

"Put the leaves [of rosemary] under thy bedde and thou shalt be delivered of all evil dreams."

Banke's *Herbal*, 1525

MARJORAM

Origanum

On the shelves used to be bundles of sweet marjoram and pennyroyal and lavender and mint and catnip ... the odorous echoes of a score of dead summers linger yet in those dim recesses.

Oliver Wendell Holmes, *A Song of Other Days*, 19th century

THESE AROMATIC HERBS—BOTH SWEET AND WILD MARJORAM—FIRST GREW AROUND THE MEDITERRANEAN AND ARE CLOSELY RELATED TO EACH OTHER, BOTH BEING ORIGANUMS. Sweet or knotted marjoram has a gentle perfume, which the 16th-century apothecary John Gerard described as "marvellous sweet." It was reputedly created by Aphrodite (the Greek Venus) as a symbol of happiness, and according to mythology, grew extensively in her garden on the slopes of Mount Olympus. Virgil described how Venus used the plant's healing powers to cure Aeneas when he was wounded in the Trojan War.

Wild marjoram is more commonly known as oregano, and its name is derived from the Greek words *oros* and *ganos,* meaning "joy of the mountain." In classical times, it was called the herb of happiness. Dittany, the origanum grown on Crete, was dedicated to the moon in mythology, and so to the goddess Diana. Legend has it that a youth named Amaracus in the service of King Cinyras of Cyprus stumbled while carrying a jar of precious perfume and dropped it. He was so afraid of the king's anger that he lost consciousness. The gods in their mercy turned him into the sweet-smelling plant that bore his name—*Amaracus dictamnus.*

In ancient Egypt, marjoram was dedicated to the god Osiris, and was woven into crowns and worn during sacred rites. The birthday flower for June 1st, marjoram stands for blushes in the language of flowers, and is described as an herb of Mercury under Aries.

LOVE & DEATH

With marjoram knots, sweetbrier and ribbon-grass,
And lavender, the choice of every lass,
And sprigs of lad's-love, all familiar names
Which every garden through the village claims.

John Clare, *The Shepherd's Calendar*, 1827

The Greeks and Romans used marjoram to crown young lovers, and the herb was woven into the coronets and wreaths worn by bridal couples at their weddings. Often included in love potions and love salves, marjoram was reputed to have a soothing effect on hesitant lovers. The Roman goddess Juno was the protector of all women, but particularly of married women. Under the name of Lucina, she was responsible for the well-being of mothers and babies during childbirth. Lucina was often depicted wearing a crown of dittany, the origanum grown on the island of Crete.

Paradoxically, marjoram was also associated with death, and was placed on burial tombs and grown on graves to give peace to departed spirits. If the herb thrived, this was a sign that all was well with the dead. It was thought that witches hated marjoram because the herb offered protection against their spells, and had the power to drive away ghosts and goblins.

Make a heart-shaped love sachet of fine cotton and fill it with dried marjoram. Place the sachet so that it perfumes the notepaper on which you write to your sweetheart.

Throw marjoram over the threshold of your home to keep the devil away.

ORIGANUM love pillow

Lightly crush and mix together some dried marjoram, woodruff, agrimony, and southernwood. Add 2 drops of marjoram essential oil if the scent is not very strong. Cut two identical pieces of cotton or linen, large enough to slip under your cheek. Sew the pieces together, enclosing the herbs, and lie with your head on the pillow to sleep soundly and dream of love.

HEALING & COMFORT

Bind your brows with the flowers of sweet smelling marjoram.

Catullus, 1st-century BC poet

THE ANCIENTS LOVED THE SCENT OF SWEET marjoram. They added it to bath water for its relaxing properties, and they massaged the oil into their foreheads and hair. Marjoram was a popular strewing herb in the Middle Ages, and its antiseptic qualities were much used in times of plague. The herb was constantly in demand for making nosegays, sweet bags, pomanders, and perfumed washing waters. The dried herb was put into bags and hung among linen and clothes to keep moths and other flying insects away. The fresh leaves and juice of marjoram were rubbed over furniture and floors to give an aromatic sheen, and the herb was also used to perfume soap.

The Anglo-Saxons used marjoram in a headache plaster, and thought that the herb was beneficial for coughs. Marjoram was highly esteemed in physic gardens, and grown prolifically for use in herbal medicines. Mixed with honey, it was applied to the skin to remove bruises, and an aromatic oil was extracted from the herb to treat stiff joints and aching muscles. Marjoram juice was thought to relieve toothache, and a marjoram, sage, and rosemary mixture boiled in wine was used as a paste to paint over black teeth. The flowers of the herb were made into a strong, hot infusion and inhaled to ease tightness of the chest, and the dried leaves were used as snuff to relieve a stuffy nose.

Marjoram, with its health-giving properties, was a favorite salad herb in the 16th century, and by the 18th century had become one of the popular sweet herbs used with meats. In stormy weather, marjoram was placed near pails of fresh milk to preserve its sweetness and stop the milk from curdling. Grown in Tudor and Stuart knot gardens, these aromatic herbs attracted bees and butterflies.

FRAGRANT sugar

To make this 16th-century recipe, add the chopped buds and flowers of wild marjoram to a jar of sugar. Stand the jar in the sun for 24 hours. Use the sugar in cake recipes and desserts for its unique aroma and flavor.

Gargle with an infusion of marjoram leaves to ease a sore throat.

Add fresh, chopped marjoram to plain scones and serve them with casseroles and stews.

PARSLEY

Petroselinum crispum

Quit the stalks of parsley hollow,
Hollow, hollow ...

Jean Inglelow, *The High Tide on the Coast of Lincolnshire*, 1863

In Greek mythology, parsley was said to have sprung from the spilled blood of the infant Archemorus, whose name meant "herald of death." The legend told how the child was laid on the ground for a nap by his nurse, and was subsequently killed by a serpent. Hercules chose this herb for the first garland he ever wore. It was customary for the victor of the Isthmian games to be adorned with a crown of dried and withered parsley, whereas the victor of the Nemean games had one made of fresh parsley.

This herb was used in folk medicine through the ages and was first mentioned in an early Greek herbal written in the 3rd century BC. The ancient Romans thought that parsley could cause pregnant women to miscarry, and this belief may explain the later custom of eating large quantities of parsley three times daily when attempting to end an unwanted pregnancy. Parsley has long been a favorite culinary herb. The Emperor Charlemagne had cheese flavored with parsley seed delivered to him every year, and Henry VIII enjoyed parsley as an accompaniment to meat and fish dishes.

Its name is derived from *petros,* the Greek for "rock," and *selinum*, meaning "parsley," and was reputed to have been so-named by Dioscorides, a Greek physician living at the time of Nero. Parsley is the birthday flower for October 30th. In the language of flowers it stands for festivity, feasting, and useful knowledge, and according to herbalists and astrologers is under the dominion of Mercury.

LOVE & DEATH

At Sparta's Palace twenty beauteous mayds
The pride of Greece, fresh garlands crowned their heads
With hyacinths and twining parsley drest
Graced joyful Menelaus' marriage feast.

Theocritus, 3rd-century BC poet

THE GREEKS LINKED PARSLEY WITH HAPPY events, and often used the leaves in bridesmaids' garlands at wedding ceremonies. At Greek feasts, the god of banquets was crowned with parsley, and guests bedecked themselves with wreaths or crowns of the herb to stimulate the appetite. They believed that this was conducive to peace and tranquility, and helped to create a serene atmosphere.

Paradoxically, this herb also came to symbolize death. It was associated with Persephone, Queen of the Dead, and the early Christians dedicated parsley to St. Peter, who was thought to be the guide for the souls of the dead. The Greeks called it the herb of oblivion. They decorated their tombs with it, and used the herb to decorate the bodies and graves of the dead. Victors at funeral games were adorned with parsley wreaths.

The herb became synonymous with death, so that a dying person was commonly referred to as "being in need of parsley." The herb acquired such an ominous significance that when a Greek army, marching into battle, encountered a mule-train laden with parsley, there was widespread panic among the soldiers. They assumed that the meeting foretold their own deaths. The term "Welsh parsley" described hemp rope, and if someone were threatened with Welsh parsley, he or she was in danger of being hanged.

Eat parsley seeds daily to increase your fertility and virility.

Include sprigs of parsley in a funeral wreath for a loved one.

QUEEN PERSEPHONE'S parsley

Prepare a mixture of finely chopped parsley and garlic or shallots. Stir this into meat and vegetable dishes just before serving to improve their flavor and color.

A FULSOME FLAVOR

I cannot tarry: I knew a wench married in the afternoon as she went to the garden for parsley to stuff a rabbit; and so may you sir; and so adieu, sir.

William Shakespeare, *The Taming of the Shrew*, 1595–1596

RICH IN NUTRIENTS, THIS HERB WAS GIVEN TO ROMAN GLADIATORS BEFORE A CONTEST to give them added strength and cunning, and Homer recounted how warriors fed their horses parsley to increase their stamina. Shepherds had a high regard for the herb, and fed their sheep on parsley for two or three hours twice a week. They believed that it gave the meat a delicate flavor, and that it also protected against foot-rot. Parsley has been a popular salad herb throughout the ages. It was included in a 14th-century recipe for a salad found in *The Forme of Cury* (1390), one of the earliest known English cookbooks.

Parsley was an important ingredient in sauces in medieval times, when its pungency and tartness helped to mask the taste of old, rancid, or salty food.

To the Hebrews, parsley is a symbol of the coming spring and of human redemption, and there is usually a dish of parsley at the Jewish Passover Feast. In the Japanese Festival of the Seven Herbs, celebrated on the morning of January 7th, orthodox Japanese eat rice broth flavored with seven herbs, one of which is parsley.

Use parsley as an appetizer before meals to stimulate the gastric juices.

Chew parsley seeds to counteract the effects of too much alcohol.

PARSLEY pie

"This may be made of veal, fowl, or calfs' feet, but the latter partley cooked first; scald a cullender full of fresh parsley in milk, season it with salt, pepper and nutmeg, add a teaspoonful of broth, and pour it into a pie dish, over the meat. When baked, pour in ¼ pt [100 ml] of scalded cream."

Anne Cobbett's *The English Housekeeper*, 1851

CURIOUS CUSTOMS

Fried parsley will bring a man to his saddle and a woman to her grave.

Traditional adage

THERE ARE MANY CURIOUS SUPERSTITIONS AND SAYINGS LINKED TO growing parsley. Some people believed that only a witch could grow it successfully, and that to ensure a fine harvest of the herb, the seeds had to be sown on a Good Friday or by a pregnant woman. Parsley is notoriously slow to germinate, and it was thought that the seed had to go back and forth to the devil seven or nine times before it sprouted. According to folklore, parsley only flourished in gardens where the mistress of the house was the master. It was believed to be unlucky to transplant parsley or to give it away, and anyone who mentioned a person's name while picking the plant condemned him or her to sicken and die. Children were told that they had been born in their mother's parsley bed, and a naive and gullible person was also described as having been born in a parsley bed.

This herb was credited with some magical powers. People believed that parsley structurally weakened glass, and that if a glass was washed in parsley water and then touched lightly it would shatter. To dream of parsley was thought to indicate unhappiness in love, but to dream of eating parsley presaged good news.

Beware: any woman who sows parsley, other than the mistress of the house, will become pregnant.

Pick parsley during a thunderstorm to increase its potency if you are using it as part of a herbal cure.

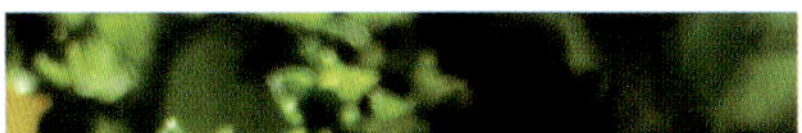

FRIED parsley garnish

Large bunch of curled parsley
Oil for frying

Wash and dry the parsley thoroughly. Heat the oil until hot enough for frying. Lower a few sprigs at a time into the frying pan or skillet, and allow the parsley to cook for about three minutes. When the sprigs are crisp, brittle, and bright green, lift them out carefully and drain on a paper towel. Serve the fried parsley immediately as an accompaniment for fried filets of fish.

CORIANDER

Coriandrum sativum

... when the children of Israel were returning
to their homeland from slavery in Egypt,
they ate manna in the wilderness
and the manna was as coriander seeds.

The Bible, Exodus XVI:31

CORIANDER WAS CULTIVATED MORE THAN 3000 YEARS AGO AND USED BY MOST ANCIENT CIVILIZATIONS. Seeds have been discovered in Egyptian tombs of the 21st Dynasty (1085–945 BC), and it was one of the medicinal plants deciphered on 8th-century Babylonian tablets. The name of this herb is derived from the Greek word *koris,* which means "bed bug," presumably because the herb smells of the insect. Coriander stands for concealed merit in the language of flowers. It is the birthday flower for December 12th and is under the influence of Saturn.

LOVE & DEATH

Coriander, Sweet pomander

John Skelton, 15th–16th century

THE HASHISH SELLER IN *THE ARABIAN NIGHTS* used this herb in his favorite love charm. An old European herbal stipulated that coriander induced love but only if the herb was gathered under a waning moon. It was believed that a woman wishing to conceive should bind 11 or 13 coriander seeds to her left thigh. Coriander was used to ease labor pains and to treat disorders of the reproductive system, and a pregnant woman would eat coriander in the belief that this would make her child witty. The ancient Egyptians placed coriander in burial tombs to protect the souls of the dead, and the ancient Chinese thought that the herb bestowed immortality.

❀ Put whole coriander seeds in wine or add crushed coriander seeds to hot coffee to stimulate passion. ❀

LUCKNOW curry powder

1 oz (25 g) coriander seed
1 oz (25 g) ginger
1 oz (25 g) cardamom seed
¼ oz (8 g) cayenne pepper
3 oz (75 g) turmeric

Grind all of the ingredients to a powder and mix together. Store in a dry place and add to vegetables or meat to make a delicious curry.

LAVENDER

Lavandula officinalis

The smell [of lavender] hidden in the green
Pour'd back into my empty soul and frame
The times when I remembered to have been
Joyful and free from blame.

Alfred Lord Tennyson, *The Ballad of Dunoon*, 19th century

LAVENDER WAS CULTIVATED BY THE ANCIENT EGYPTIANS IN THE SACRED WALLED GARDEN AT THEBES. They prized the herb greatly, using it to make a soothing and healing balm that was part of the ritual of mummification. It was turned into an expensive perfume to adorn both the living and the dead. Perfume urns were sealed into tombs to provide fragrance, and when Tutankhamen's tomb was excavated, the scent of lavender was still strong even after 3000 years. In ancient Greece, virgins who were being sacrificed to the gods were decorated with lavender flowers, and essence of lavender was used to perfume the breath of courtesans.

Until fairly recently, this distinctive herb was highly prized as a flavoring for a variety of culinary dishes, both savory and sweet. The herb became so popular that fields of hazy blue flowers were a frequent sight throughout Europe, and lavender maids were seen in busy streets selling the herb whenever it was in season.

The herb was a popular edging plant for knot gardens in Tudor and Elizabethan times, and it even became fashionable to have a lawn of lavender instead of green grass. Moira Castle in Ireland was well-known in the 17th century for its vast lavender lawn of more than an acre. Lavender is the birthday flower for January 9th. Lavender stands for constancy in the language of flowers, and in the ancient floral vocabulary it symbolizes silence.

LOVE

Lavender is for lovers true

Elizabethan lyric

LOVERS OFTEN GAVE EACH OTHER A GIFT OF lavender as a symbol of affection. Charles I courted Nell Gwyn with bags of dried lavender tied with gold ribbon. It was customary to perfume wedding clothes with the herb, and Irish brides wore a garter of green lavender for good luck. However, if you seek a lover, beware—according to the old wives' saying, lavender will only grow in an old maid's garden. There was a popular belief that if a young girl wished to remain chaste, she should dry some lavender flowers and sprinkle them on her head.

LAVENDER love cookies

4 oz (100 g) butter
2 oz (50 g) superfine sugar
6 oz (175 g) all-purpose flour
2 tsp lavender buds

Cream the butter and sugar together until light and fluffy. Add the sifted flour and lavender buds, reserving a few for later. Mix together and knead to form a smooth dough. Roll out on a lightly floured board and cut with a heart-shaped cutter. Sprinkle the remaining buds on top. Bake on a greased tray at 325°F (160°C/gas mark 3) until firm to the touch and golden in color. Cool on a wire tray.

♥ Keep a small sachet of dried lavender against your bare skin to attract a lover. ♥

♥ Hide sprigs of lavender in books when separated from a lover. After some time, check their color and perfume to reveal the strength of your lover's feelings. ♥

♥ Rub the flowers off lavender heads to use as confetti at a wedding. ♥

Passion potpourri

Sprinkle lavender, rose, and patchouli essential oils over a mixture of lavender flowers, rose petals, a cup of fresh or dried vervain leaves, and orris root. Place by the door of your bedroom. Each time you enter, stir the potpourri with the ring finger of your left hand (the vein leads straight to the heart) and you will find that love will flourish there.

COMFORT

LEGEND TELLS US THAT MARY WASHED Jesus's swaddling clothes in lavender water, and this may be one reason why the herb has been popular for laundering throughout history. For the Greeks and Romans, lavender was a favorite ingredient of bath extracts. It was used to make fragrant soaps, soothing balms, and comforting tinctures. In Elizabethan times, lavender was popularly added to soap to give clothes and linen a fresh perfume, and as a result, a laundress became known as a *lavendre.* St. Hildegarde, a Benedictine abbess who grew lavender in her garden in the 12th century, is often credited with the invention of lavender water. Elizabeth I is reported to have paid dearly for a lavender and gillyflower-scented water.

Roman women put lavender flowers in brackets carved in bedposts to deter bed bugs, and they massaged lavender oil into their scalps to protect against head lice. For centuries, lavender was strewn around houses to ward off invading insects. Scraps of material were soaked in lavender oil, encased in a thin cotton bag, and hung in rooms to keep them free from flies. Lavender was distilled and put on dusters to give furniture a fragrant sheen, and nosegays were hung around houses to mask unpleasant odors and the more pungent medieval smells from the streets. The expression "to lay in lavender" is a colloquialism for pawning, because pawned clothes were often strewn with lavender to keep them smelling sweet.

Velvet gown and dainty fur
Should be laid in lavender
For its sweetness drives away
Fretting moths of silver-grey.

Constance Isherwood,
***A Bunch of Sweet Lavender*, 1900**

♥ Relax the mind and body at bedtime by placing lavender pillows on the bed and hanging bunches of lavender around the room. If you are feeling particularly stressed and tense, vaporize some lavender essential oil in an oil burner for an hour before retiring. ♥

♥ Drink an infusion of lavender flowers at night to calm the nerves and make you feel drowsy. ♥

♥ Make a fragrant lavender bag using dried lavender flowers, dried rosemary leaves, chopped orris root, and rose essential oil. Keep it in your purse to refresh you when traveling. ♥

Sleep remedy

"For they that may not sleep, seep this herb [lavender] in water and let him soak well his feet to the ankles at bedtime and bind it on the temples, and he shall sleep well by the Grace of God."

Antony Ascham, *The Little Herbal*, 1525

HEALING

Aunt Jobiska made him drink lavender water tinged with pink
For she said: The World in general knows
There's nothing so good for a Pobble's toes!

Edward Lear, *The Pobble with No Toes*, 1871

LAVENDER HAS LONG BEEN USED IN FOLK medicine, particularly for easing stiff joints and relieving tiredness. It was a popular treatment for headaches, and Elizabeth I, who suffered from migraines, was known to drink up to 10 cups of lavender tea daily to relieve her fretful brow. Lavender water was used as a gargle to ease toothache, restore a lost voice, and calm the tremblings and passions of the heart. In the 19th century, no respectable lady left the house without a small vial of lavender cologne in her purse to revive her in the event of a sudden attack of the vapors.

This herb had a reputation for repelling the plague. It was noted that the glove makers of Grasse, who used lavender oil to perfume their leather, enjoyed remarkably good health and remained free from infection during an epidemic. This probably started the custom of carrying lavender during times of plague. The powerful antiseptic action of oil of lavender was employed to treat skin complaints, and was used to disinfect and dress wounds during World War I.

♥ Ease stiff joints by massaging lavender essential oil lightly over affected areas. ♥

♥ Spray lavender water onto the skin as an insect repellent when on vacation. ♥

LAVENDER nightcap

"I judge that the flowers of lavender quilted in a cap and worne are good for all diseases of the head that come from a cold cause and that they comfort the braine very well."

William Turner, *New Herbal*, 1551

SWEET BASIL

Ocimum basilicum

Herbs too, she knew, and well of each could speak
That in her garden sipp'd the silv'ry dew ...
The tufted basil, pun-provoking thyme,
Fresh balm, and mary-gold of cheerful hue.

William Shenstone, *The Schoolmistress*, 1742

LEGEND HAS IT THAT BASIL GREW AROUND THE TOMB OF JESUS AFTER THE RESURRECTION. However, in Greece there was a belief that the Empress Helena found basil growing at Golgotha, the site of the Crucifixion, and then took the herb back to Greece. Some Greek Orthodox churches still use basil in the preparation of holy water, and adorn their altars with the herb. It was traditional for Greek men to attach sprigs of the bright green herb to their hatbands when they went to church on Stavros Day, September 14th—the Day of the Cross.

In India, basil has always been revered as a plant of great sanctity. It was known as the sacred herb *tulasi,* and was dedicated to the gods Vishnu, Krishna, and Siva. Basil was held in such reverence that solemn oaths in a court of law were sworn on it, and every village home had its own basil bush. Good fortune was thought to await Hindus who built their homes where basil had once thrived, but misfortune would come to anyone who wantonly uprooted the herb. In Russian mythology, basil was associated with a youth named Vasili, who was famed for his exceptional beauty, but in Crete the herb was considered a plant of ill-omen and linked with the devil. Basil is the birthday flower for July 12th. In the ancient floral vocabulary it symbolized poverty, probably because poverty was often depicted as a woman clothed in rags standing or sitting beside a basil bush. Astrologers ruled that it was an herb of Mars, under the influence of Scorpio.

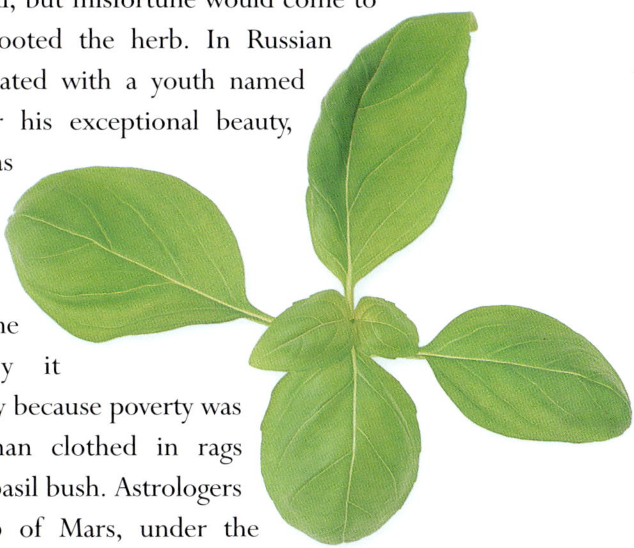

LOVE & DEATH

Madonna, wherefore hast thou sent to me
Sweet basil and mignonette?
Embleming love and health which never yet
In the same wreath might be.

Percy Bysshe Shelley, 19th-century poet

TO THE ROMANS, BASIL WAS A HERB OF fertility, and they believed that it would only flourish where it was tended by a beautiful young maiden. The herb was linked with the handsome god Krishna in the Hindu faith and therefore became associated with love. In Tudor England, it was customary to give little pots of basil as love tokens, and in Greece a sprig of basil was offered to guests as a sign of welcome. The heart-shaped leaves of basil were love tokens in Italy. It was believed that if a girl accepted a sprig of the herb from a suitor, she would fall madly in love with him, and if a man took a shoot of fresh basil from a woman, he would love her forever.

In India, it was believed to be unlucky if a death occurred in a house, so a dying Hindu would be carried outside and placed under a basil bush. After death, the body was buried with a sprig of basil on the breast, in the belief that the herb would act as a passport to paradise. In ancient Egypt, the women who visited the tombs to pray for the souls of the dead would scatter an offering of basil around the sepulchers.

♣ Put a pot of basil in your window to signify that you are expecting a visit from your lover. ♣

♣ Cultivate a healthy basil bush to have a steady stream of admirers. ♣

CHILDBIRTH pain reliever

This ancient advice was reputed to ensure pain-free childbirth:

"... a woman in labour if she hold in her hand a root of this herb [basil] together with the feather of a swallow, shall be delivered without pain."

HEALING

Fine basil desireth it may be her lot,
To grow as the gilliflower, trim in a pot,
That ladies and gentles to whome ye do serve
May help her, as needeth, poor life to preserve.

Thomas Tusser, 16th-century poet

Basil has been used in folk medicine since ancient times. The Greeks and Romans chewed basil leaves as a tranquilizer, and included the herb in potions to calm the digestive system. It was used both as an expectorant and as a laxative. In 16th-century Europe, an infusion of basil was a popular treatment for catarrh. The herb was also turned into snuff to ease inflamed mucus membranes and to alleviate migraine headaches. Some medics thought that basil was good for uplifting the spirit and clearing the brain.

The Japanese used basil tea to treat the symptoms of the common cold, and in India, a decoction of basil was taken to help troublesome coughs. The leaves were sometimes chewed as a betel substitute to stimulate the flow of saliva. Early herbalists believed that basil could draw out the poison from scorpion stings, and the herb was used as a household cure for bites and insect stings. However, some physicians were reluctant to prescribe basil, and the 17th-century herbalist Nicholas Culpeper recorded that the herb "either makes enemies or gains lovers there is no in-between."

♣ Sip a cold infusion of basil leaves to prevent motion sickness. ♣

♣ Crush a basil leaf and rub the juice onto your skin to repel mosquitoes. ♣

♣ Put a few drops of essential oil of basil into your bath water for a refreshing and revitalizing effect. ♣

♣ Drink a hot infusion of basil leaves last thing at night to prevent a cold from developing. ♣

TONING muscle rub

Basil leaves
Coarse sea salt
Olive oil

Put several layers of the ingredients in a jar and seal. After a few weeks, strain off the oil and use it as a muscle rub.

FLAVOR & FRAGRANCE

With basil then I will begin,
Whose scent is wondrous pleasing.

Michael Drayton, 16th-century poet

Fragrant basil was grown in the gardens of Rome at the time of the Caesars. It was introduced to Western Europe much later by the spice traders, and then to North America and Australia by early European settlers. Basil has not always been popular as a culinary herb, although it was included in a 14th-century French recipe for a green pickle, and was mentioned as an herb suitable "for pottage" in a 15th-century English manuscript. However, by the 17th century it had become a popular seasoning, and was used in London at that time to give a characteristic flavor to the famous Fetter Lane sausages made there. In the 19th century, Francatelli, Queen Victoria's cook, used basil for the special seasoning he invented.

In medieval times, basil was a general room freshener, being popular as a strewing herb to keep away insects. It was a component of nosegays, tussie-mussies, pomanders, and the bouquets of mixed flowers and herbs called bough-pots or beau-pots. It was also made into scented water for bathing.

HEAVENLY pesto

4 oz (115 g) Parmesan or pecorino cheese, cubed
4 oz (115 g) pine nuts
1 oz (25 g) fresh basil leaves
2 cloves garlic
3 fl oz (75 ml) olive oil

Blend all of the ingredients together to produce a puree. Add salt, if desired.

♣ To ensure a good crop of basil, curse the seeds as they are being sown. ♣

♣ Preserve freshly chopped basil in a little water frozen in ice-cube trays. Use in your cooking as required. ♣

A loving cup

"About the end of August fill a wide-mouthed bottle with fresh leaves of basil, cover with Sherry, and infuse them 10 days; strain and put in fresh leaves, infuse another 10 days, then pour off, and bottle it."

Anne Cobbett, *The English Housekeeper*, 1857

THYME

Thymus vulgaris

For he painted the things that matter,
The tints that we all pass by,
Like the little blue wreaths of incense
That the wild thyme breathes to the sky.

Alfred Noyes, *The Elfin Artist*, 20th century

According to legend, thyme was one of the fragrant herbs used for the bed of the Virgin Mary, and this probably explains why it is called the herb of motherhood. In herbal lore, it was thought that thyme grew from Helen of Troy's tears, but this herb was in fact known and used long before the Trojan War, and was one of the herbs ritually burned as incense on altars to the gods of ancient Greece and Rome. The generic name *Thymus* came from the Greek word *thumos,* meaning "courage," and this herb was linked with courage in the folklore of many cultures. Roman soldiers bathed in thyme-scented water to give them courage and added vigor during battle, and to the Greeks, also, thyme symbolized bravery.

During the Middle Ages, a sprig of the herb was given by a lady to her knight when he left for the Crusades, and the knight would wear it as a symbol of strength. Another popular farewell gift was a scarf embroidered with a sprig of thyme. This denoted loving remembrance. In the 15th century, during the English War of the Roses, this custom continued, and Lancastrian ladies gave their knights embroidered favors with a bee hovering over the herb. In the south of France, before the French Revolution, wild thyme was a symbol of republicanism, and to receive a sprig of thyme meant that you were summoned to a republican meeting. Once thought sacred to Mars and Venus, this robust, sun-loving herb is the birthday flower for June 9th. In the ancient floral vocabulary, thyme stands for spontaneous emotion or activity.

LOVE, DEATH, & MAGIC

And in his left hand he held a basketfull
Of all sweet herbs that searching eye could cull:
Wild thyme, and valley-lilies whiter still
Than Leda's love …

John Keats, *Endymion*, 1818

ACCORDING TO FOLKLORE, IF A YOUNG WOMAN PLACED a sprig of thyme in one of her shoes and a sprig of rosemary in the other, on the Eve of St. Agnes (January 20th) she would see a vision of her future husband. Thyme was also a popular component of a lover's nosegay. Throughout the ages, this herb has also been associated with death. In Wales, people believed that thyme gave refuge to the souls of the dead, particularly those who had met a violent death, and there are many instances recorded of the smell of thyme lingering near the place where a murder had been committed. The ancient Egyptians used this plant as an ingredient in the fluid with which they embalmed the dead. Thyme has also been associated with witchcraft and magic. It was used by the Anglo-Saxons in their "nine herbs charm," and an early 17th-century recipe in the Ashmolean Museum in Oxford, England, records thyme as one of the ingredients of a magical ointment used to see fairies. Fairies and elves were believed to be particularly fond of wild thyme.

❖ Beware: according to folklore, if a toddler is the first person who touches a thyme plant when it has just been planted in an herb garden, he or she will remain single for life. ❖

❖ It is considered unlucky to have thyme in the house for fear that it will cause death or illness to a member of the family. ❖

TALL tales

After telling a story of love, death, or magic, finish with this old saying:

My tale's ended,
T' door sneck's bended;
I went into t' garden
To get a bit o' thyme;
I've telled my tale,
Thee tell thine.

HEALING & COMFORT

The opening summer, the sky,
The shining moorland—to hear
The drowsy bee, as of old,
Hum o'er the thyme.

Matthew Arnold, *Haworth Churchyard*, 1855

THYME HAS HAD MANY USES IN POPULAR medicine. The Romans infused it as a tea to treat melancholy, and considered it a good remedy for a hangover. Thyme was included in a 1st-century preparation to aid digestion, and bruised thyme leaves were used as an antidote to bee stings. The Greeks and Romans fumigated rooms by burning thyme, a custom that helped to repel fleas and other insects.

In Elizabethan England, an infusion of thyme and ground ivy was thought to ease inflammation of the uterus or breasts, and to help expel the afterbirth. The 17th-century herbalist Nicholas Culpeper recommended the herb as a sure remedy for nightmares. Thyme was thought to cure coughs, colds, and disorders of the bowel and bladder, and it was believed to improve eyesight and clear the brain. In the reign of Queen Anne in England in the early 18th century, thyme and beer soup was thought to cure shyness. Herbalists prescribed thyme blossom for healing wounds and relieving gout, and believed that a strong thyme decoction stimulated hair growth and prevented dandruff.

❖ Put a sprig of thyme under your pillow for pleasant dreams. ❖

❖ Add thyme essential oil to your bath water to ease rheumatic pains. ❖

❖ Macerate 3 handfuls of thyme in 8 fl oz (250 ml) brandy. Store and use it as an effective—and very pleasant—toothpaste or mouthwash. ❖

ANTISEPTIC inhalation

2 pints (1 liter) boiling water
4 drops thyme essential oil

To relieve a stuffy nose, pour the boiling water into a bowl. Add the oil. Put a towel over your head to contain the steam, and breathe in the decongestant fumes deeply for about 10 minutes. After treatment, rest for half an hour in a warm place.

FLAVOR & FRAGRANCE

... wind-bit thyme that smells like dawn in Paradise ...

Rudyard Kipling, 19th–20th-century writer

THYME HAS BEEN A FAVORITE ingredient in the kitchen throughout the ages, and was cultivated for its culinary properties in the ancient gardens of Assyria and Babylon. The Greeks and Romans used thyme to flavor cheese and liqueurs, and loved thyme-scented honey. The honey produced by bees on Mount Hymettus in Greece and on Mount Hylba in Sicily was particularly famous, and in 17th-century England, beekeepers were instructed to plant thyme near hives to attract bees. The ancients encouraged sheep and goats to graze on wild thyme because they thought it had a beneficial effect, adding flavor to the animals' meat as well as to their milk.

Thyme was a popular hedging plant in European herb gardens, and was one of the plants clipped low to form a neat border for knot gardens. Creeping varieties were used to make lawns, paths, and mats in front of garden seats, so that the aroma of the herb was released when walked on; thyme still grows rampantly in the famous gardens at Sissinghurst Castle, England. To smell of thyme was a compliment in ancient Greece, so after bathing, Greeks included oil of thyme in their daily massage. Virgil said that the highest praise a shepherd could give to his mistress was to say that she smelled of thyme.

THYME-flavored oil

8 sprigs of thyme
2 garlic cloves
8 black peppercorns
8 juniper berries
25 fl oz (700 ml) virgin olive oil

Put all of the ingredients into a glass bottle, seal tightly, and shake well. Set the sealed bottle in a sunny place for three weeks before using, shaking the bottle frequently to bring out the full flavor of the herbs.

❖ Plant thyme near lavender in your herb garden to help both plants flourish. ❖

❖ Use dried thyme as an aromatic moth repellent in cupboards and drawers. ❖

BERGAMOT

Monarda didyma

[Bergamot] should be propagated plentifully in the kitchen garden for the sake of the leaves, to afford tea which is highly agreeable and refreshing.

William Hanbury, 18th-century rector

THIS FRAGRANT PLANT WAS DISCOVERED BY THE EARLY SETTLERS IN NORTH AMERICA. It was named after the Spanish physician and botanist Dr. Nicholas Monardes, who wrote a book in the 16th century describing the flora of America. After the Boston Tea Party in 1773, when the American colonists revolted against import duties levied by the British Parliament by emptying the contents of tea chests into the harbor, they used wild bergamot to make Oswego tea or Liberty tea. By the 19th century, bergamot tea had become popular in England, too.

LOVE & COMFORT

Speak not—whisper not,
Here bloweth thyme and bergamot,
Softly on thee every hour
Secret herbs their spices shower.

Walter de la Mare, 19th–20th-century poet

IN ENGLISH FOLKLORE, BERGAMOT ACQUIRED A reputation as an herb of fertility, and as recently as the 19th century, the herb formed part of every bride's dowry in the hope that it would prove beneficial to the young mother-to-be. This herb was also used in cosmetics. It was mixed with citrus oils and lavender to make Eau de Cologne Imperiale, named after the Empress Josephine. Napoleon, who loved its perfume, included it in his daily toilette, and poured it over his neck after washing, even when he was on military campaigns.

❊ Enjoy a relaxing herbal bath by steeping 2–3 tbsp fresh bergamot leaves in boiling water for 10 minutes. Strain and pour the liquid into your bath water. ❊

LOVERS' potpourri

1 cup dried bergamot flowers and leaves
3 cups dried rose petals
1 tbsp orris root powder

Put all of the ingredients in a pretty container by your bed, or use it to fill a sleep pillow.

Citrus bergamia is a small, bitter orange tree that grew around the town of Bergamo in northern Italy, after which bergamot was named. Both plants have similar scents.

SAGE

Salvia

The wholesome sage and lavender still gray,
The roses reigning in the pride of May ...

Edmund Spenser, *The Fate of the Butterfly*, 16th century

TO THE ANCIENTS, THE SALVIA FAMILY OF HERBS HAD POTENT MAGICAL POWERS. The Greeks believed that sage could render a man immortal, and the Egyptians worshipped it as a giver and saver of life. The Romans revered the herb so much that harvesting it was accompanied by special rituals. Sage could only be cut by clean, barefoot gatherers dressed in white tunics and using special bronze or silver tools. Prior to harvesting, ceremonial sacrifices of food and wine were made to the gods. In Crete, where the herb grew prolifically, it was traditional to gather sage on the first or second day of May before the sun had risen. In medieval times, the plant was believed to have been blessed by the Virgin Mary, and earned the synonym *Officinalis Christi*. The name sage was derived from the Latin *salvare*, meaning "to heal," and because life-saving powers were attributed to the herb, it was sometimes called *Salvia salvatrix*, meaning "sage the savior."

Curiously, the health of a sage plant was thought to reflect the business fortunes of the master of the house. A thriving plant indicated a flourishing business, but a withered plant suggested that all was not well financially. Ancient physicians extolled sage's healing and fortifying properties, both for the body and for mental functions. Sage is the birthday flower for January 19th. In the ancient floral vocabulary it symbolizes esteem, and in the language of flowers it signifies domestic virtue. According to the 17th-century herbalist Nicholas Culpeper, sage is an herb of Jupiter.

LOVE & DEATH

If the sage bush thrives and grows,
The master's not master and he knows.

Traditional adage

THERE WAS A CURIOUS BELIEF THAT SAGE only prospered in the gardens of the wise and wherever the wife ruled the household. Sage leaves were often used as love oracles. If a young woman went into the garden at midnight on All Saints' Eve (Halloween, October 31st), and picked nine sage leaves without breaking the branch just as the clock was striking, she would see the face of her future husband, or the image of a coffin if she was destined not to marry.

Both the Romans and the Egyptians considered sage to be a potent fertility drug. Childless couples who wanted to conceive were advised to remain apart for four days, while drinking sage juice daily—when intercourse recommenced, conception was almost ensured!

In folklore, sage was thought to ease grief, and was a plant commonly planted on graves as a sign of remembrance. The 17th-century diarist Samuel Pepys wrote of "a little churchyard, where the graves are accustomed to be all sowed with sage."

Hang a sprig of sage in a window when a loved one goes on a journey. If the sage remains fresh, the absent person is well.

Snip off sage flowers in the garden before they open to avoid misfortune.

Brush some sage over anyone suffering from nightmares to expel evil spirits.

SAGE advice

According to 17th-century herbalist Nicholas Culpeper, women who have difficulty in conceiving should take:

"the juice of sage with salt, 4 days before they company with their husbands, it will help them to conceive."

HEALING & COMFORT

Rue is nothing in comparison to sage
Sage preserved the human race

Alphonse Karr, 19th-century writer

SINCE EARLY TIMES, SAGE HAS BEEN LINKED with longevity and strength. According to one old Arabic saying: "Why should a man die who has sage in his garden?" An old English proverb recommended eating sage in May in order to live a long life. People believed that sage improved the memory, and they drank sage tea as a tonic for the mind and body.

The ancient Romans made sage wine to cure various ailments, and sage seeds were crushed in water and used as a poultice for swellings. In the Middle Ages, sage was prescribed to treat colds, fevers, cholera, and the plague. The 17th-century herbalist Nicholas Culpeper commented that "the juice of sage drunk with vinegar hath been of good use in the time of the plague." It was one of the herbs used in the celebrated four thieves' vinegar with which people tried to make themselves immune to infection during times of pestilence. Since the 17th century, sage has been used for dental hygiene, and the leaves were rubbed on the teeth and gums.

Nicholas Culpeper

Eat seven sage leaves on seven consecutive mornings before breakfast to cure a fever.

Make an infusion of sage tops and China tea, and use it as a rinse to restore natural color to hair that is turning gray.

Eat sage in May to live to an old age.

SAGE salve

"For the Itch—Take a pound [450 g] of butter, unwashed and unsalted, three good handfuls of red sage, and as much brimstone [sulphur] beaten into powder as a walnut, boil these well together, and strain it and put in half an ounce [15 g] of ginger beaten small."

Jane Mosley's *Derbyshire Remedies*, 17th–18th century

FLAVOR & FRAGRANCE

There in the front grows sage, sweetly scented
It deserves to grow green forever, enjoying perpetual youth
For it is rich in virtue ...

Wilafred Strabo, 9th-century monk and poet

THE ROMANS USED SAGE SEEDS TO FLAVOR cheese, and in Russell's *Boke of Nurture* there is a recipe for sage fritters, a favorite dish in the Middle Ages. The Emperor Charlemagne so loved the flavor of this robust herb that he ordered that sage should have pride of place in his gardens. Sage tea became popular in China in the 17th and 18th centuries. The Chinese prized sage tea so much that they traded the Dutch three chests of tea leaves for each chest of sage leaves.

A popular strewing herb because of its antiseptic properties, sage was used to repel insects and vermin around the house. It was also used in nosegays and tussie-mussies. A posy made of chamomile flowers surrounding a sprig of sage signified wisdom and the serenity of years, and was carried by elderly ladies.

Plant sage next to beehives for a fragrant sage-flavored honey.

Blend chopped sage into wholegrain mustard, and smear the paste over meat before roasting or barbecuing for a special flavor.

POWERFUL **punch**

"Take Western sage blossoms, which must be gathered thoroughly dried and cured in the sun, and pack them into an empty pint [600 ml] bottle to the depth of two inches [5 cm] or more. Add to this the peel of one lemon which has been detached from its fruit and thoroughly dried in the sun. Fill the bottle to the top with good bourbon, and let stand for at least two weeks before using ... the longer the better."

Mrs. Lackner's *Mountain Bitters*

TANSY

Tanacetum vulgare

Fragrant the Tansy breathing from the meadows
As the west wind blows down the long green grass.

John Clare, 19th-century poet

ACCORDING TO MYTHOLOGY, ZEUS FELL IN LOVE WITH GANYMEDE, A YOUNG MORTAL MAN OF EXCEPTIONAL BEAUTY, AND CARRIED HIM OFF TO MOUNT OLYMPUS. In order to make Ganymede immortal, he was given a potion of tansy to drink. Thereafter, he became cup-bearer to the gods. The name tansy comes from the Greek *athanasia,* which means "immortal." Tansy is the birthday flower for February 23rd, and according to astrologers is associated with the planet Venus. In the language of flowers it means "I declare war against you."

LOVE & DEATH

[Tansy] is [a woman's] best companion, the husband excepted.

Nicholas Culpeper, 17th-century herbalist

FROM MEDIEVAL TIMES ONWARD, TANSY WAS used to help women conceive. The bruised leaves were also applied to the navel and a tansy infusion drunk to treat a threatened miscarriage. It was traditional in England for young men and women to offer tansy cakes as forfeits in an Easter game that involved trying to steal the buckles from each other's shoes. In ancient times, tansy oil was believed to have preservative powers. It was smeared on dead bodies to stop them from decaying, and bunches of the herb were enclosed in the shrouds of corpses to prevent them from being eaten by maggots.

❤ Wear tansy leaves in your shoes as a charm against misfortune. ❤

SWEET & SOUR **tansy**

To make this medieval recipe, fry tansy leaves, green corn, violets, and eggs together. Serve the omelette to your lover with an orange and some sugar to sweeten a sour mood.

MARIGOLD

Calendula officinalis

The marigold that goes to bed with the sun,
And with him rises weeping.

William Shakespeare, *A Winter's Tale*, 1610–1611

The pot marigold has strong associations with early Indian and Arabic cultures. The Indians venerated the herb and used it to decorate temple altars, shrines, and statues of their gods. To the Hindus, it represented life, eternity, and health. A Greek legend tells the origin of the flower. A young maiden named Caltha fell in love with the sun god and only lived to see him reappear each day. As she watched each morning for the sunrise, she was consumed by her passion and finally wasted away. To commemorate her devotion, the first marigold appeared on the spot where she had carried out her daily vigil. The marigold was said to be a favorite flower of the Virgin Mary, who wore it on her breast—hence, the name Mary-gold.

In heraldry, this herb symbolizes devotion and piety. It was the favorite flower of Marguerite de Valois, grandmother of Henry IV of France, and she chose an emblem of the flower turning toward the sun as her coat of arms. Huguenot soldiers, before going into battle, would pick a marigold from her garden and wear it to denote their allegiance.

Marigold is the birthday flower for January 15th. In the dictionary of flowers, it stands for grief and jealousy, but in the language of flowers it depicts a sunny disposition. According to the 17th-century herbalist Nicholas Culpeper, the marigold is an herb of the sun under Leo.

LOVE & DEATH

The ancient Greeks bedecked themselves with marigold garlands at wedding feasts. This herb was considered to be a lucky plant to have in the house, and its bright yellow flowers, which were thought to reflect the sun, were believed to be protective. To dream of the herb signified prosperity, success, or a happy marriage. However, the 14th-century poet Geoffrey Chaucer linked the flower with jealousy when he depicted the figure of jealousy wreathed in marigolds. In Tudor times, it was fashionable for ladies at the English royal court to wear wreaths or carry bouquets of marigolds intertwined with heart's ease (pansies), and Anne Boleyn loved to adorn herself in this way. Sometimes marigolds were included in various love potions and love charms, and were often used by young people in different forms of "loves-me, loves-me-not" rhymes.

The ancient Hindus used this bloom to adorn funeral pyres, and Shakespeare also referred to the marigold as a funeral flower. A combination of marigolds and poppies in a tussie-mussie (posy) held the message "I will soothe your grief," and a wreath of marigolds and cypress was a traditional token of despair. Native Mexicans called this plant the death flower, because they believed that each flower sprang from the life-blood shed by their countrymen when the Spanish settlers landed there in search of gold.

Look! the constant marigold
Springs again from hidden roots.

Robert Graves, 20th-century poet

❋ Touch marigold petals with your bare feet to be able to understand what the birds are saying. ❋

ST. LUKE'S love salve

On St. Luke's Day (October 18th), mix together some marigold, thyme, wormwood, honey, and white vinegar. Use the salve to anoint the breasts, hips, and stomach while lying in bed and repeating the words:

St. Luke, St. Luke,
be kind to me
In dreams let me
my true love see.

FLAVOR & COLOR

Long before rising time, when duckshooters
Haunted the marigolds and bull rushes ...

Seamus Heaney, 20th-century poet

THROUGHOUT HISTORY, THE MARIGOLD HAS been used to flavor and color food. In the kitchen, fresh petals and young leaves were added to salads, and in 16th-century Europe, it was fashionable to float the fresh and dried flower heads on soups and stews. The English essayist and critic Charles Lamb, recalling the unappetizing meals at Christ's Hospital during his student days there in the late 18th century, wrote disparagingly of this custom:

... boiled beef on Thursdays ...
with detestable marigolds floating in
the pail to poison the broth.

Marigold petals, which contain a coloring substance called calendulin, were used in place of saffron to add color to rice and give it a slightly peppery flavor, and they were also used to color cheese and butter. The green leaves were sometimes served with spinach as a vegetable. Marigold flowers were used in drinks, especially possets, and to make marigold wine. The fresh flowers were preserved for winter use by drying, pickling, or candying.

❋ Stand a bunch of marigolds in the kitchen to absorb cooking smells. ❋

❋ Dry the petals to add color to potpourris. They are particularly effective when mixed with green leaves. ❋

❋ Use a ring of small, even-sized marigold heads to decorate an iced cake. ❋

CALENDULA custard

3 tbsp marigold petals
¾ pint (450 ml) milk
2 tbsp sugar
½ tsp vanilla essence
2 large eggs

Pound the marigold petals in a mortar. Blend all of the ingredients together, and pour into individual ramekin dishes. Stand the dishes in a shallow tray of water and bake at 285°F (140°C/gas mark 3) for approximately half an hour until the custards are lightly set. Garnish with an individual marigold flower head.

HEALING

Open afresh your round of starry folds,
Ye ardent marigolds.

John Keats, 19th-century poet

THE ANCIENTS BELIEVED THAT MARIGOLD could drive evil thoughts out of the head, and Macer's 12th-century herbal advised that just looking at the herb improved the eyesight, cleared the head, and encouraged a cheerful disposition. The marigold is referred to in a 13th-century medical manuscript, and seems to have been used mainly to combat the plague at that time.

Throughout the ages, marigold has been used for treating toothache, varicose veins, for relieving the pain from burns, scalds, and stings, and as a digestive medicine. It was prescribed for cases of smallpox and measles. In Jamaica, a marigold decoction was popular for starting delayed menstruation and for treating other female disorders. During the American Civil War, marigold leaves and the juice from the flowers were used to treat open wounds and to stop bleeding from deep cuts. During World War II, both the leaves and the flowers were employed in a medicine to promote sweating and treat bronchial complaints. Desert tribesmen of the Middle East prepared a strengthening elixir for their stallions and brood mares from marigold flower heads. They thought that this made the foals stronger and faster.

❋ Apply a cooling compress of marigold flowers to minor burns and scalds. ❋

❋ Use the sap from marigold stems to treat corns and warts. ❋

❋ Make an infusion of the flowers to induce sweating to relieve a fever. ❋

MARIGOLD moisturizer

2–3 tbsp marigold petals
¼ pint (100 ml) boiling water
4 oz (115 g) unscented moisturizing cream

Prepare a strong infusion by steeping the marigold petals in the boiling water. Heat the moisturizing cream slightly, then whisk in the strained marigold infusion. When cool, apply the cream to areas of rough skin.

INDEX

Page numbers in *italics* refer to illustrations

aches and pains 19, 48
Achilles 21
Adonis 53
aggression, provoking 30
ague 48
air purifier 26
alcohol, counteracting 86
Alfonso, King of Castile 33
Alfric, Archbishop 68
All Saints' Eve 114
Amaracus 79
angelica 24–7, *24*, *25*
Anglo-Saxons 8, 41, 47, 81, 104
Anne, St. 47
antiseptics 19, 29, 32, 42, 76, 81, 95, 106, 117
aphrodisiacs 29, 42, 68
Aphrodite 53, 79
Apollo 15, 16
Arabs 73, 121
Archemorus 83
Aristotle 42, *42*
Artemis 35, 57
asthma 48

babies, protecting 22, *22*
baldness 57, 76
Barbarossa, Emperor 59
basil 96–101, *96*, *99*
bay 10, 14–19, *14*, *15*, *17*
beau-pots 101
bed bugs 94
bees, attracting 43
bergamot 19, 108–9, *108*, *110–11*
bites 19, 25, 35, 48, 61, 100
bladder disorders 106
bleeding 23, 37, 61
blood 45
blood pressure, high 23, 61
Book of Changes 22
borage 62–5, *62*, *63*
bough-pots 101
bouquet d'église 47
bowel disorders 106
boyfriends, getting rid of 30
breath, sweetening 43, 91
broken hearts 21
bronchial complaints 125
broomsticks *11*, 16
bruises 81
bullfighters 30
burns 125

Caltha 121
catarrh 100
Catherine of Aragon 35
chamomile 19, 46–9, *46*, *47*, *50–1*
Charlemagne, Emperor 55, 83, 117
Charles I 92
chastity 92
Chaucer, Geoffrey 122
chervil 37, 44–5, *44*
chicken pox 68
childbirth 19, 42, 45, 57, 89, 98, 106
children, calming 68
Chinese 22, 37
Chiron 35
chives 36–7, *36*, *38–9*
cholera 116
Christmas 10, *10*, 18
Cinyras, King 79
Circe 29
Claudius, Emperor 16
colds 23, 48, 76, 100, 106, 116
compresses 11
conception 114, 117
constancy 91
coriander 88–9, *88*
corns 125
coughs 61, 76, 100, 106
courage 30, 64, 103
cramps 61
Crete 97, 113
crossroads 29, 47
Culpeper, Nicholas 8, *8*, 15, 100, 106, 114, 116, *116*
cunning 86
curses 60, 67, 68
cystitis 48
dandruff 106
Daphne 15
death 16, 80, 84, 98, 104, 119
decoctions 11
Delphi 15
demons 8, 54
dental hygiene 116
depression 48
devil 60, 80, 97
diabetics 27
Diana 35, 79
digestive troubles 48
dill 55, 66–9, *66*, *67*, *68*
Dioscorides 61, 67, 83
disease 8, 10, 19
disinfectants 26, 57, 60
double vision 9, 41, 45
dreams 23, 30, 74, 80, 87, 106, 122
Druids 9, 22
drying herbs 10

earache 42
Eau de Carmes 27
Egyptians 32, 33, 47, 48, 57, 67, 89, 91, 98, 104, 113
Elizabeth I 94, 95
Elizabeth II 49
Elizabeth, Queen of Hungary 76
embalming 71
evil (spirits) 8, 16, 22, 29, 30, 37, 54, 60, 114
exhaustion 35
expectorant 100
eyes 48
eyesight 30, 53, 54, 61, 106, 125
eyewashes 45

face, dry skin 64
fairies 9, 22, 104
faithfulness 18
farewell gifts 103
female disorders 48, 125
fennel 8–9, *8*, 35, 52–5, *52*, *53*
fertility 84, 98, 109, 114
fever 22, 23, 48, 61, 64, 116, 125
fines herbes 37, 45
fingernails 69

fleas 106
foot bath 42
"four thieves' vinegar" 32, 116
fumigation 106
funerals 71, 74, 84, 122
future, foretelling 22

Galen 32
gangrene 48
Ganymede 119
garlic 27, 28–33, *28*, *29*, *31*
Gerard, John 8, 79
ghosts 54, 80
gladiators 53, 86
good luck charms 16, 21, 30
gout 76, 106
graves 47
Greeks 15, 18, 29, 33, 43, 61, 69, 73, 80, 83, 84, 91, 94, 97, 100, 103, 106, 107, 113, 121, 122
grief 114, 121
gripe water 68
gums, sore 23
Gwyn, Nell 92

Hades 41
hair 49, 106, 116
Halloween 114
hangovers 106
harvesting 9
hayfever 48
head lice 94
head sores 42
headaches 61, 67, 76, 81, 95, 100
healing 6–8, 13
Hebrews 33, 86
Hecate 29, 41
Helen of Troy 103
Helena, Empress 97
Henry VIII 35, 83
heraldry 59, 121
herb gardens 7, 10, 107
herbals 6–8
Hercules 83
hiccups 42, 45
Hildegarde, St. 94
Hinduism 97, 98, 121, 122
Holy Saturday 18
holy water 97
Homer 63, 86
Huguenots 121
hysteria 48

I Ching 22
immortality 89, 113, 119
India 97, 98, 100, 121
indigestion 68
infectious diseases 19
inflammations 61
infusions 11
inhalations 48, 106
insect repellents 10, 43, 57, 117
insecticides 19
insomnia 48, 68, 94
Isis 57
itching 116

Japanese 86, 100
jaundice 30
jealousy 121, 122
Jesus Christ 73, 94, 97
John, St. 22, 47, 54
Juno 80

knot gardens 91, 107
Krishna 97, 98

Lamb, Charles 124
laundry 76, 94
lavender 57, 90–5, *90*, *91*, *93*
laxative 100
legs, tired 64
Leonardo da Vinci 61
lepers 32
life, prolonging 25
lightning 16, 47
limbs, aching 19
linen, perfuming 81
longevity 116
Louis XIV 63
love oracles 114
love potions 54, 68, 71, 80, 122
love salve 122
love tokens 98
lovers 92
lovesickness 64
loving cup 101
Lucina 80
luck *see* good luck charms
lust 25
madness 60
magical herbs 8–9
malaria 48
Marguerite de Valois 121
marigold 120–5, *120*, *121*, *123*
marjoram *11*, 78–81, *78*, *79*
measles 125
medical treatises 6
Meetin' House seeds 55, 69
melancholy 106
memory 61
menstruation 125
Michael the Archangel, St. 25
Michaelmas 25
Michelangelo Buonarroti 61
Midsummer 8–9, 22, 41, 47, 54, 74
migraine 23, 95, 100
mint 40–3, *40*, *41*, 57
Minthe 41
miscarriage 83, 119
moisturizer 125
moly 29
Monardes, Dr. Nicholas 109
monasteries 6, 27, 42
Moses 45
mosquitoes 100
moth repellents 81, 107
motion sickness 100
mouthwashes 23, 43, 106
mummification 91
murder 104
muscles 48, 61, 81, 100

Napoleon 109
New Year 18
nightmares 8, 106, 114
nosebleeds 23, 61
nosegays 81, 101, 104, 117

Odysseus 29
oregano 79
Osiris 79

Parkinson, John 8, 25
parsley 37, 82–7, *82*, *83*, *85*
passion 89
pennyroyal 41
Pepys, Samuel 114
Persephone 41, 84
Peter, St. 84

physic gardens 6, 81
plague 10, 16, 25, 26, 32, 81, 95, 116, 125
planting herbs 9
Pliny 53, 57, 61, 63, 67
Polo, Marco 33, 37
pomanders 43, 81, 101
Portuguese 55
posies 37, 49, *49*, 71
potpourris 10, 92, 109, 124
pregnancy, unwanted 83
Prometheus 53
purging 19
purifier 26
Puritans 55

recipes 11
rejuvenation 25
religious festivals 13
remembrance 10, 73, 114
rheumatic pains 19, 106
Romans 18, 29, 33, 35, 43, 48, 53, 61, 67, 69, 73, 80, 83, 94, 98, 100, 103, 106, 107, 113, 117
rosemary 10, *10*, 19, 57, 72–7, *72*, *73*, *75*
rue 58–61, *58*, *59*
Russia 97

sacred herbs 8
sage 112–17, *112*, *115*
St. Agnes' Eve 104
St. John's Day 41, 47, 54
St. John's Eve 8–9, 22, 74
Saturnalia 18
scalds 125
second sight 61
sexual powers 54
shipwreck 30
shyness 106
sickness 22
sight, restoring 30
Siva 97
skin cleanser 49
sleep, inducing 43, 48
smallpox 125
smells, absorbing 124
snuff 43, 100
sorcerers 67, 68
sore throat 81
spells 60, 67, 68
stamina 86
stings 19, 35, 45, 61, 100, 106, 125
stomach upsets 42, 61, 68
storms 47
strength 86, 116
stress 94
strewing 10, 19, 43, 49, 54, 55, 60, 81, 101, 117
sty, bathing 48
success 18, 53
swellings 116

talismans 9, 30
tansy 118–19, *118*
tarragon 34–5, *34*, 37
Thousand and One Nights 42
thrush 48
thunder 16, 47
thyme *8*, 9, 54, 102–7, *102*, *103*, *105*
Tiberius, Emperor 16
tiredness 43
toilet water 26, 43, 76
tongues, rough 42
tonics 32, 49, 116
toothache 32, 81, 95, 125
toothpastes 43, 106
tranquilizer 100
tuberculosis 48
tussie-mussies 37, 49, *49*, 101, 117, 122

vampires 29, 30
varicose veins 125
Venus 79
vertigo 61
Virgil 79, 107
Virgin Mary 63, 73, 94, 103, 113, 121
virility 84
Vishnu 97
vomiting 19

warts 30, 125
weather, divining 22
weddings 23, 43, 54, 71, 74, 80, 84, 92, 122
weevil beetle 19
"Welsh parsley" 84
wet nurses 64
whooping cough 32
witches:
- broomsticks *11*, 16
- detecting 60
- keeping away 22
- protection against 8, 9, 26, 30, 60, 67, 68, 80
- spells and potions 9, *9*, 13, 22, 41, 45, 57, 104

wormwood 9, 56–7, *56*
wounds 21, 32, 48, 106, 125
wreaths 10, *10*, 18, 122
wrinkles 45

yarrow 20–3, *20*, *21*
Yarrow Stalk Oracle 22
youth, preserving 76

Zeus 119

CREDITS

All photographs were provided courtesy of:

Flowers & Foliage

with the exception of:
page 7: Sylvia Corday
page 8 (top) & page 9: Image Select/Ann Ronan
page 10 (left), page 12 (top right), & page 29: Quarto

Author's Acknowledgment

This book is dedicated with my dearest love to Colin, Kerry, and Bryone.